Doing Development –

Governments, NGOs and the Rural Poor in Asia

Doing Development –

Governments, NGOs and the Rural Poor in Asia

edited by Richard Holloway

Earthscan Publications Ltd
London

in association with CUSO

First published 1989 by
Earthscan Publications Limited in association with CUSO
3 Endsleigh Street, London WC1H 0DD

British Library Cataloguing in Publication Data

Doing development: governments, NGOs and the rural
  poor in Asia.
  1. Asia. Rural regions. Economic development
  I. Holloway, Richard
  330.95′0428

ISBN 1 85383 034 8

Typeset in 10/12pt Palatino
by Photoprint, Torquay, Devon

Printed and bound in Great Britain
by Cox & Wyman, Reading, Berks

Earthscan Publications Ltd is an editorially independent and
wholly owned subsidiary of the International Institute for
Environment and Development.

Cover incorporates detail of photomontage *Skyscrapers* by Thurman Rotan
(1932). Inset by Mark Edwards/Still Pictures: Refugees from Bangladesh
living in the centre of Calcutta.

Richard Holloway has spent his whole working life in the Third World (and quite a lot of his younger years living there as well). He has worked for both government and non-government organizations on development programmes in Ethiopia, South Sudan, Botswana, the Eastern Caribbean, the South Pacific, Indonesia, and has been most recently the Regional Field Officer for the whole of Asia for CUSO, a Canadian development organization. He is presently living and working in Bangladesh.

Location of Organizations and Programmes

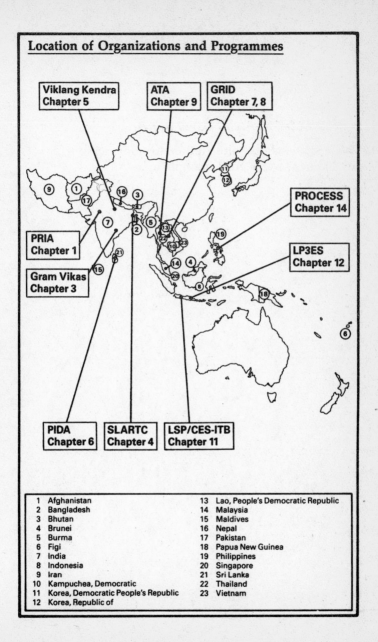

Viklang Kendra Chapter 5

ATA Chapter 9

GRID Chapter 7, 8

PROCESS Chapter 14

LP3ES Chapter 12

PRIA Chapter 1

Gram Vikas Chapter 3

PIDA Chapter 6

SLARTC Chapter 4

LSP/CES-ITB Chapter 11

1 Afghanistan	13 Lao, People's Democratic Republic
2 Bangladesh	14 Malaysia
3 Bhutan	15 Maldives
4 Brunei	16 Nepal
5 Burma	17 Pakistan
6 Figi	18 Papua New Guinea
7 India	19 Philippines
8 Indonesia	20 Singapore
9 Iran	21 Sri Lanka
10 Kampuchea, Democratic	22 Thailand
11 Korea, Democratic People's Republic	23 Vietnam
12 Korea, Republic of	

to Robert Chambers and David Korten

whose knowledge of and attitude towards doing development was a great example to me.

Contents

SOUTH-EAST ASIA

Doing Development –

Governments, NGOs and the Rural Poor in Asia

Foreword

There are three observations which are fundamental to the implementation of development programmes in Asia during the 1980s:

(i) The absolutely poor, who are mostly rural people, are a significant (not a marginal) part of the population of all developing countries in Asia. In some cases their numbers are increasing.

(ii) Many (perhaps most) of the development programmes implemented by governments (and assisted and advised by the bilateral and multilateral donors) have damaged the position of the very poor people in the rural areas. They have done this by making them even poorer and more powerless in relation to the rest of the society. This has been most acute in the case of rural women. None of this has been the intention behind the development programmes but it has been the result, achieved by sustaining, reinforcing and encouraging existing social and political structures that exploit the poor.

(iii) The non-government sector (people's movements, religious organizations, NGOs (non-government organizations) and universities) has devised an "alternative" development strategy whose programmes are specifically intended to empower the powerless and selectively enrich the poorest. Such programmes are, however, of very limited scope compared to those implemented by national governments.

In order to improve the lives of the rural poor in Asia, development programmes must be devised which recognize both the unequal and exploitative nature of existing social and political structures, and the latent capacity of the rural poor to develop themselves once the constraints have been removed.

NGOs have the commitment and the experience; national governments have the means and the resources. There are, however, many complicating factors which stand between the synthesis of these two elements into viable programmes to help the poor and powerless. This book tries to illustrate some of the differences between government and NGO programmes and some of the difficulties they experience in working together. In some of the cases discussed here, the differences are explicit while in others, the authors concentrate on the singular nature of the NGO programmes, and the implicit differences between them and those run by governments. My intention is to open the eyes of the reader to the qualitative limitations of government programmes and the quantitative limitations of NGO programmes. Finally, I would like to suggest ways in which both of these limitations can be overcome.

In this foreword I want to introduce the pertinent elements of the debate. I will give the background to the contributing articles in the Preface. The articles themselves will illustrate, through the experiences of the various organizations, the different contexts in which the debate has been joined. In the Afterword I suggest how things could be improved.

The established government development paradigm[1]

The established paradigm is to increase production and create growth, and to do this against a background of increased national (or at any rate the present govern-ments') security. Government efforts to achieve growth have been directed towards those on whose loyalty they can count, and whose resources can be mobilized. Thus, government policies have been intended to develop those with land, collateral and resources to invest, and with the assumption that their greater wealth will benefit the whole society. Many government programmes have been successful in these aims and the richer peasants and middle classes have indeed grown wealthier, but at the expense of those who are already poor. The rural surpluses have been extracted by rural élites and townspeople while the objections of the poor to this process have been contained or controlled in the name of "security".

Those who start off by being "resource poor" have had very little involvement in development planning and planned growth. Not surprisingly, the growth-oriented policies and programmes have not impinged on their lives very much. In some cases, such programmes have actually been harmful to them and may have even taken away the small amount of resources they had – such as land.

Within the official paradigm of production, growth and security there have been some programmes which have had the express (though generalized) intention of helping the poor. Such programmes have been based (either overtly or implicitly) on the following assumptions:

(i) The rural poor are a homogeneous group, all the members of which can respond equally well to the opportunities offered by development programmes, and all of whom have the same economic and social constraints.

(ii) Planning for rural development programmes is best done by urban-based experts, usually male.

(iii) The most suitable development programmes are those which will involve agro-businesses (and cash crops for export) and will include the introduction of technologies, ideas and structures from more developed countries.

(iv) The participation of the rural poor in the development plans is necessary, but is to be limited to their collaboration in the plans produced by outside experts.

(v) The governments (and their advisers) know best about development programmes and the rural poor will be best advised to participate in the plans their government makes for them.

The rural poor thus become the "objects" of development programmes devised by others, and are not given the opportunity to contribute their knowledge and skills to the process. Indeed, their knowledge and skills are rarely recognized. Not surprisingly, therefore, programmes with these assumptions have rarely managed to empower or enrich the rural poor in the long term.

I have assumed that "development programmes" actually intend to help the poor in the first place. A more cynical view would point out that the empowerment and enrichment of the poor was never the final aim. Asia has long been characterized by nation states ruled autocratically by people who are not themselves from the poorest classes; government programmes are carried out by officials within centralized and hierarchical structures; élites control the social and economic world of the poor, and have close connections with government officials whose programmes have enriched them; and the élites and the government officials are both disdainful of the knowledge and capabilities of the poor.

In these circumstances it is not surprising that, in many cases, the programmes devised simply do not fit the economic, political and social situation of the rural poor, even if (with the best will in the world) they were intended to do so. In many cases, there is nowhere near the best will in the world, but a tacit and cynical acceptance that benefits will not "trickle down", but will be *filtered out* by the rural élites. In some instances, this passive acceptance will be a positive intention.

Even in cases where, due to good research and good judgement, programmes have been devised which "fit" the world of the rural poor, they have never been "owned" by the people. On the contrary, they have been imposed on them from the top by people whose motives may legitimately be considered suspect by the poor.

The non-government organizations paradigm

Groups outside government have tried a number of initiatives intended specifically to help the poor and the powerless change their lives. These deal more realistically with their situation than government programmes. An analysis of the experience and achievements of such groups gives us the following "alternative" assumptions about programmes for the rural poor, based on a different development paradigm:

(i) The poor and powerless are kept that way by social and economic structures which dominate rural society. Any assistance which does not specifically address the conditions which keep people poor and powerless will end up by being filtered out by the rural élites. Similarly, assistance which does not specifically address the particular problems of women is likely to be filtered out by men.

(ii) The poor know what structures dominate their economic and social lives, but are only willing to talk about them if they are convinced that such openness will not prove harmful. Special efforts are needed to persuade poor people that they can initiate and organize their own development, and participate in decisions about their own livelihood. Special efforts are also needed to protect them if their initiatives make them vulnerable.

(iii) All the countries referred to in this book have an economy directed mainly by market forces and the capitalist mode of production. Ideas, structures and technologies imported from capitalist countries will, not surprisingly, be most relevant to those with capital and who deal in the cash economy. Most rural poor are subsistence farmers who sell any surplus. Their access to the cash and capital necessary for participating in technological advances only comes by the means of exploitative structures (usually money-lenders), and so their ability to benefit in the long term from the introduction of technology is limited. While centrally planned economies do not have the same problems, it is interesting that they share with capitalist countries, the same heavy-handed approach to "top-down" programmes for the poor.

It is of much more use to the poor to ensure that their own skills, knowledge and resources are employed and to keep this capacity to use them alive. An important part of this process is for outsiders to recognize the value of indigenous knowledge, to collect it systematically, and to incorporate it into development programmes.

The ideas put forward by the Asian NGOs are the most pertinent to changing the lives of the poor and the powerless for the better. For many years now, the NGOs have been implementing their ideas as alternatives to the government programmes and their experience has shown how valuable these ideas are. Sadly, these ideas are often seen by governments to be subversive when they should, on the contrary, be recognized as pioneering efforts which warrant further study and wider replication. The work of

NGOs has often been insignificant, *ad hoc* and unsustainable, and NGO practitioners are often inexperienced in dealing at the national-policy level. On the other hand, governments and their advisers are coming to appreciate that, even with these faults, NGOs have valuable experience which they would be ill-advised to ignore.

Government departments

While it is tempting to set government and non-government organizations in opposition to each other, it must be said that Asian governments are not monolithic and some of their departments work outside the received and dominant development wisdom. They also often publicly subscribe to the view that NGOs and government should work together. The reality is not, however, so simple.

Enlightened government departments do indeed have opportunities to help the poor and powerless, but experience has shown that low-level government functionaries who actually interact with the poor in administering government programmes find the "alternative, NGO-type" kind of development a threat to their status and livelihood and do not encourage them. There often seems to be a gulf between an official government statement and the actual behaviour of local functionaries who make some part of their living by controlling access to government services.

Some government departments do identify new areas of work which are pertinent to the poor and powerless (e.g., community forestry, sustainable agriculture, appropriate technology and the community rehabilitation of the disabled) and some of the processes they use give the beneficiaries a say in the design of the programmes.[2] With due caution given to checking the ways in which the programmes are implemented, such work can often be worthwhile and should be supported. My experience has led me to believe, however, that there is often a wide gap between rhetoric and reality.

Among development observers there is often a naïve and false optimism that governments will adopt some of the methods and experience of the NGOs. In some cases this does actually happen, but a more realistic view will appreciate that there are two different approaches to "development" at work, and that national governments and their functionaries are likely to lose personal power and income (if not face) by subscribing to the other way of working. If this *is* the case, we can expect token and face-saving gestures, but little real change.

Peoples' movements and NGOs can try to confront these unhelpful attitudes, demand their legal and constitutional rights, and clearly oppose corrupt and exploitative attitudes and programmes. Culturally, this seems an attractive strategy to the peoples of South Asia and the Philippines. On the other hand, the history of the peoples of South-East Asia (apart from the Philippines) has made them well aware that confrontation with the state usually produces a violent and self-defeating backlash. They seem temperamentally more inclined to work from within and try to effect change more silently, by creating coalitions of like-minded people and gradually building up a consensus which will change policies.

One way or the other, by confrontation or by consensus, there are forces both inside and outside Asian governments which are pushing them to become more effective in helping the poorest in their societies. Similarly, there are forces inside and outside NGOs which are pushing them to become more widely effective. Each side is likely to be working more with the other in the years ahead but the possibility is also very real that each side may be unable to accept the other's strategy and practice – governments may become more repressive and poor citizens may turn in desperation to revolution. This book illustrates some of the contexts in which programmes for the rural poor happen in Asia, and how both governments and NGOs approach them, and sometimes work together.

Richard Holloway
Penang, Malaysia

October 1988.

NOTES
1. Another, similar, explanation of the dominant paradigm, but in more macro-economic terms, can be found in Susan George, "A philosophical afterword" in *A Fate Worse than Debt* (Penguin Books: Harmondsworth, 1988), p. 255.
2. These have been documented in Norman Uphoff, *Local Institutional Development: An analytical sourcebook with cases* (Kumarian Press: West Hartford, Connecticut, 1986).

Preface

This book was assembled from the experiences of NGOs (non-government organizations) in Asia with which CUSO,[1] a Canadian development agency, has been associated. The only exception is Joe Madiath's contribution (Chapter 3) which has been included because it is such a clear illustration of what happens to government programmes specifically intended to benefit the poor.

The pieces chosen illustrate the topics which CUSO, in collaboration with its Asian partners, decided to make the focus of their support in Asia. They range from agriculture to the disabled, but are all founded upon the strong belief that the best development for the poor will come from removing the invalid and irrelevant programmes currently being thrust upon them, and devising plans for their future in which they are involved and in which they have some say.

One of the main methodologies used in realizing this belief has been "Participatory Action Research". It is illustrated in the articles by Ponna Wignaraja (Chapter 2), S.P. Wickramaratchi (Chapter 6), Janet Durno on GRID (Chapter 7), James Terrent and Hasan Poerbo (Chapter 11), and Rafael S. Espiritu (Chapter 13). This methodology is carried out in different ways in different places but in all cases aims to make the rural poor the subjects of their own development, rather than the objects of other people's plans.

In most cases, the pieces are written by Asians who are personally involved in the work described. In others, I have not had such work to draw on and the articles are written by CUSO staff (myself and Janet Durno). Most of the articles describe programmes which have dealt (and still deal) with both men and women in the poorer communities taken together – there are few which are gender specific. Recognizing, however, the particular added difficulties which the female poor face, I have included an article on a programme of legal rights for women in India (SLARTC, Chapter 4), and an article on the place of women in a generalized community organizing programme in Thailand (GRID, Chapter 7).

Another specific programme with which CUSO has been concerned is the strengthening of indigenous self-reliance. The article on the work of the Appropriate Technology Association (ATA) in Thailand with sustainable agriculture is an example of this (Chapter 9). It starts with the cultivation of rice and fish together in the paddy field and moves on to a whole new (or perhaps old) integrated agricultural system that allows Thai people in the North-East to be self-sufficient in food rather than having to make up a regular annual deficit by seasonal migration to the towns.

• •

NOTES
1. CUSO Asia is one of the six regional offices of CUSO, originally the Canadian University Services Overseas organization. It has sub-offices in Bangladesh, Thailand and Indonesia and has been active in Asia since 1961. In its early years it was concerned with the placement of Canadian volunteers, but has in the last decade focused more on the support of Asian NGOs.

1. The State and Voluntary Agencies in Asia

by Rajesh Tandon

Rajesh Tandon is the Director of the Indian organization Participatory Research in Asia (PRIA), as well as head of the Asian Secretariat for the Participatory Research Group of the International Council for Adult Education. PRIA has been involved in helping Indian NGOs to manage themselves and their relations with the Indian government which has, in the current Five Year Plan, recognized and made provision to assist NGOs. There is much dispute amongst Indian NGOs as to whether this represents an attempt to co-opt and finally to control them or not. This chapter was an internal document of PRIA that has been circulated amongst Indian NGOs in order to stimulate discussion.

The growing debate about Indian voluntary agencies, their role and contribution, clearly shows the new social reality of this historical juncture. Any discourse on voluntary agencies needs to take into account the character of the state and its relations with voluntary agencies. After independence, India is called a liberal democracy. Unlike military dictatorships or single party states, the situation of liberal democracies is rather complex. In such a set-up, the state had begun to play an increasingly important role in the area of development. Non-government organizations have played a variety of complex roles; sometimes collaborating with the state, its agencies and officials in order to plan and implement particular development programmes. They have also questioned the role of the state

The Central Problem

Source: Richard Holloway and David Watson (eds), *Changing Focus – Involving the Rural Poor in Development Planning* (Oxford and IBH Publishing: New Delhi, 1989).

in perpetuating existing inequality and injustice which tends further to marginalize the poor and the oppressed.

It is in these situations that the role of NGOs and their relationship with the government becomes most interesting.

It has been generally assumed that, in a liberal democracy, the state would like to work towards the development of its people. It would like to work towards creating programmes and policies which help in improving the situation of the poor and the oppressed. However, the structure of the government, the character of the state and the penetration of vested interests in rural and urban areas, make it impossible to accept that assumption. By their very nature, liberal democracies take a pro-masses position and the political leadership of such democracies never fail in mouthing populist slogans. However, basic practice and the implementation of those policies and programmes make it very clear that the political economy of the government (the character of the state and its agents) determines the nature of development programmes and how they will be implemented, and therefore determines the consequences for the poor and the oppressed. It is in such a situation that there is a need to reconceptualize the role of NGOs and the essential philosophy that they represent, in order to determine the likely nature of their relationship with the state and its agents.

The nature of NGOs in India

The history of voluntary work in India is several decades old. During the nineteenth century, the roots of voluntarism were sown in the work of social-reform movements which began to challenge the feudal system obtaining in the country. At the time of British colonial rule voluntarism became an even more popular idea as people joined the fight for independence. In particular, the impact of Mahatma Gandhi and his philosophy further strengthened voluntary movements in the 1920s and '30s. This was evident in his call for constructive work and the way he inspired thousands of young women and men to work among the rural poor, scheduled castes,[1] and those deprived of education, health, employment and income-generation. This period witnessed the flowering of the spirit of voluntarism and the sacrifices of volunteers to the cause of socio-economic upliftment of the poor and the weak. It was also the time when India became free of foreign rule.

Around the 1950s, several voluntary organizations were established in response to the need for relief and rehabilitation of large numbers of people affected by floods, drought and other calamities. This period also saw the rise of philanthropic, charity-oriented voluntary organizations. These NGOs developed and implemented programmes to help enhance short-term gains that the poor and deprived could experience in education, income, health, nutrition and so on. From the mid 1960s until the mid 1970s, several voluntary organizations emerged which experimented with different approaches to development problems. It was then that experiments in community-health programmes led to the emergence of the concepts and principles of primary health care. It was also then that innovative localized drinking-water programmes led to the design and development of India Mark II hand-pumps as well as the popularization of traditional well-digging technology. It was also then that rural-development programmes based on local initiatives, resources, knowledge and expertise, began to be evolved. New ideas about adult education, new approaches to the preparation of learning materials, and new experiences in training also began to emerge during this period.

Though few in number, such voluntary agencies began to demonstrate, through their practice, the ineffectiveness of the prevalent model of development which till then continued to incorporate the "trickle-down" theory. They also began to throw up some alternative principles and ideas for more people-based, localized, people-controlled development strategies. From the mid 1970s, there emerged a new type of voluntary agency more appropriately called Social Action Groups. These groups were the result of rising frustration with the ineffectiveness of existing approaches and models of development in solving the pressing problems of poverty, deprivation, hunger, unemployment, and so on. It became clear that raising the consciousness of the poor and oppressed, showing them how to organize, and enhancing their collective empowerment to demand their rights and to acquire resources for their own development is perhaps the only long-term strategy of sustaining people-centred development in India. These groups, comprising small teams of four or five young women and men, sprang up in different parts of the country and began to work with the poor and the oppressed. Starting with an analysis of their existing socio-economic and political situation, they essentially focus on helping the poor to get organized, to understand their legal rights and collectively to make efforts to demand them.

At the moment, there are several thousand voluntary agencies in India, performing a wide variety of functions and roles. Almost all of the above mentioned co-exist, though many organizations contain within themselves elements of all these types. In the last six to seven years, there has also arisen a form of intermediary organization in the voluntary sector. They are involved in training, research, documentation and networking, and have helped the process of inter-organizational co-operation, consolidation, linkage and the coming together on issues of common concern. This linkage and coming together have been demonstrated in cases relating to forests, tribals,[2] women, the environment, dams, occupational

health and safety, the Bhopal gas disaster, the implementation of minimum wages, and land rights. The role of
networking and bringing grassroots activists and groups
together on issues of common concern (so that these
concerns could be shared and analysed, and so that
regional/national strategies on them could be worked out)
has gained considerable importance in the country during
the last five or six years.

Relations with the state

This account of the various types of voluntary organiza-
ions in India is a useful guide in trying to analyse the
nature of their role and its implication for the relationship
with the government. For voluntary organizations which
are involved in relief and rehabilitation programmes, and
in developing alternative ways of delivering services (in
order to provide education, health, income-generation,
afforestation, etc.), the policies and programmes of the
Indian state, in particular of the central government during
the last five or six years, can be a useful umbrella.

Such agencies have been able to acquire resources from
the state, either directly from the ministries of the central
government or state government, or through such para-
statal bodies as CAPART,[3] in order to finance their projects
and programmes. There are also voluntary agencies which
have implemented government programmes in particular
sets of villages, and these agencies have done a remarkably
more efficient and effective job. Through CAPART and
other ministeries in central government, there have
emerged in the last two and a half years, a significant
number of schemes for financing the projects and programmes of voluntary agencies within the overall policy
and programmatic framework of the government of India.
Thus, there are schemes for drinking water, housing,
afforestation, improving the lives of women and children

in rural areas, health care, adult education and literacy, which voluntary agencies can undertake. These schemes are moulded on national plans and programmes that come from central government.

It is true that while acquiring resources through these schemes and implementing the projects and programmes thus financed, voluntary agencies face a variety of hurdles and problems at the local level. The local-government officials of the village and the block (the level below the district) are invariably apathetic or hostile to voluntary efforts. They do not offer the support that is needed for the implementation of these programmes. They withhold essential information and materials without which voluntary agencies cannot undertake these programmes. Sometimes, they also withdraw or delay the necessary sanctions and approvals, causing severe hardship to voluntary agencies. Despite this, in the role of service-provider and in the implementation of development schemes and programmes, there is no inherent contradiction between the state and the NGOs.

The role of Indian NGOs in programme implementation, service delivery, relief and rehabilitation has begun to be accepted by the state as a legitimate one. This has been particularly so for the last six or seven years, more so in the context of the Seventh Plan document which explicitly recognizes the role of voluntary agencies in the realization of rural poverty-alleviation programmes. Even though, at a conceptual level, the NGOs' role in a country like India is congruent with the development orientation and promotional roles of the state, it's actual practice seems to create conflicts and tensions. It is important to recognize that any development effort entails a process of social change and, therefore, implies changes in the relationships between individuals, families, classes and sectors. If poor tribals in a forest area begin to acquire effective health care then their dependence on local touts and witch-doctors is reduced, thereby affecting the economic base of such forces in the area. Obviously, whenever the material conditions, the position of power, status, control, access to resources and information, is challenged or altered due to the interventions of a development programme, it is not surprising that those who are adversely affected attempt to resist or undermine this change.

So, at the base level of the state machinery, local-village level workers, patwaries,[4] BDOs,[5] primary-school teachers, health-care inspectors, forest guards, and a host of other local officials, tend to consider an effective voluntary agency as the source of their trouble. It is not surprising that they begin to impede the effective functioning of such agencies. However, the support and the resources that these agencies receive from central and state governments, and other para-statal organizations, ensure that a protective umbrella is provided, at a higher level in the bureaucratic structure. As a result, local intimidation, harassment and victimization caused by petty officials can be dealt with rather effectively, though at times painfully, by the voluntary organizations.

One of the roles that voluntary agencies have begun to play (as described earlier) is that of raising awareness and building up organization amongst the poor and oppressed. This is based on the recognition that the poor themselves must develop the sense of collective empowerment, understanding, knowledge, competence, and self-confidence in order to demand their own rights and thereby struggle for a process of transformation. Clearly, for such an educational and organizational role to be played by many NGOs in a country like India, is quite in opposition to the existing vested interests of the state as well as of the rural and urban élites. When a group of landless labourers understands the legally available minimum wages and the way in which to acquire them, or when they begin to demand minimum wages, local land-lords and land-owners may try to resist and may consider voluntary agencies supporting such an educational process to be the source of all this trouble. When a group of women begin to demand their just participation in the Integrated Rural Development Programme (IRDP) or DWCRA[6] programme as a consequence of the educational and organizational efforts of a local NGO, the local- and district-level officials may feel harassed, threatened or perturbed, and may point their fingers at such voluntary organizations as the cause of this problem. When a group of newly aware and organized tribals begin to resist the corruption of patwaries and forest guards, and struggle to demand what is rightfully due to them, those petty officials see it as a threat to their livelihood and tend to retaliate both against the tribals and their organizations, and the voluntary agencies working with them.

Therefore, even in a liberal democracy like India, the demand for constitutionally enshrined rights and their implementation is considered an anti-social and anti-ational act. Such attempts are politically denounced, and characterized as destabilizing and anti-national because they are perceived to hurt the political-economic interests of those currently in power. The irony of this is further accentuated when, in a country like India, the state itself creates a programme such as "Organizations of Beneficiaries". This recently created programme, funded by the state and routed through CAPART, is now being implemented by several voluntary agencies to help organize the rural poor. This is the clearest example of the inherent contradictions in the state as it now stands in a country like India today. The issue is not one of contradictions; the issue is how the state will learn to cope and react to these contradictions.

Problems in relations

In this context, the relations between voluntary agencies and government have to be situated within an overall analysis of their roles, as well as the nature of the state in the existing liberal-democratic framework. In the past, several attempts have been made at co-operation and collaboration between NGOs and state agencies and programmes.

In the early days right after Independence, the movement of community development was seen as a people's movement. Over a period of time, the government became interested in this movement and began to take over what was essentially the people's programme. The same pattern can be seen in the case of co-operatives. Historically, they have been one of the clearest expressions of the people's own initiatives and organizations for economic improvement. The state took an increasing interest in co-operatives, initially under the guise of supporting and funding them, but now state intervention and control is all-pervasive and, in many states, total. The state now has the right to appoint officers, supercede duly elected governing bodies, institute enquiries into its affairs, and merge, bifurcate or in any other way intervene in a co-operative.

The basic question in this history of relations between voluntary agencies and the government is whether or not the state has the capacity and the will to relate to voluntary agencies on the basis of mutual respect, autonomy, equality and trust. It is clear that, increasingly, the state has become an all powerful, all controlling, all resource-owning entity. In comparison, an individual voluntary agency, or even a group of them, is relatively powerless, resourceless and isolated. Therefore, to begin with, the relationship between agency and state is characterized by positions of unequal power, making it very tempting for the state to dictate conditions and terms of discourse. As a result, past moves for co-operation and collaboration by the state have been attempts to support voluntary agencies and at the same time demand their complete and total subservience and blind adherence to the overall policies, programmes and priorities of the state.

This problem gets more complicated if we look at different types of voluntary agencies and the various roles they play. The agencies for relief and rehabilitation seem to find it less painful or difficult to relate to the state, or to acquire resources from it. In recent years, service-delivery NGOs have also begun to attract a lot of support from the state and its programmes. The real difficulty comes when the agencies and agents of the state have to figure out how to relate to social-action agencies or those NGOs which are engaged in consciousness raising and organization-building among the poor and deprived. Whenever the work of a voluntary agency has led to increased questioning of the local vested interests (including those of party members), pressures have been brought to bear on the state to exert influence upon such agencies. In the face of unpleasant and opposing situations, apparently created through the actions of voluntary agencies, the machinery and agents of the state typically use three forms of response.

The state response

The first and most direct form of response is to intimidate, harass, or physically attack voluntary agencies and their staff. Examples of fieldworkers from voluntary agencies and social activists being harassed by the police, physically beaten up, and/or threatened, occur daily throughout the country with increasing frequency. The nature of this harassment could also sometimes be indirect and not necessarily physical. Intimidation and harassment by means of exploiting existing legal instruments and machinery to serve the interests of the state and its agents are also common.

The most frequent and concrete example is the abuse of the Foreign Contribution (Regulation) Act by the state and its agents. Hundreds of voluntary agencies are being denied their legitimate right of registration under the Act, without any apparent reason. Similarly, many of these agencies are being harassed by the cancellation of their registration numbers often without any proper hearing and/or substantial basis. A similar form of harassment is employed through the Income Tax Act, Wealth Tax Act, Sales Tax Act, etc. Many voluntary agencies are receiving demands for huge amounts of income-tax arrears, allegedly due from them. A third form of intimidation is to use the pretext of having received funds from the government and then initiating a series of enquiries, questions, inspectors' visits, and so on. The visit of intelligence officers to the doors of voluntary agencies has become an almost regular phenomenon. If you apply for a grant, you have to receive them; if they want to enquire into the use of your grant, they visit you. A fourth kind of harassment is the laying of false charges against voluntary agencies and their leaders. The most fashionable of these is that the agency is attempting to "convert" the people to Christianity or Islam, for instance. This has been the experience of many voluntary agencies working in tribal areas.

The basic tenet of all this is that voluntary agencies are suspect until proven otherwise. With the national paranoia of "the invisible foreign hand causing destabilization", low-level officials and clerks in various departments of central and state government have begun to believe that a voluntary agency which is receiving foreign funds is engaged in activities detrimental to national and public interests and is, therefore, suspect unless clear evidence is provided to the contrary. It is this attitude that is reflected in the manner in which these officials relate to the senior leaders of NGOs, the type of questions they ask, the language they use, and the behaviour they exhibit. All speak volumes for the intimidating and harassing thrust of the state response.

The second most common state response, and one that is used increasingly, is that of negating or undermining the value of an NGO's contribution. This is done by pretending that NGOs have not carried out any work in a particular area, or by ignoring the work that has been done or undermining its value. For example, the vast experience generated by grassroots NGOs in the areas of ecological improvement and afforestation undertaken with the involvement of the people, alternative methodologies of training, research and evaluation, income-generating programmes, etc. – all are ignored by the government staff. Many government departments, officials and agencies tend to ignore the relevance of any work that has been done by them. Thus, negation is a very powerful response to withdraw recognition and legitimacy from the contribution and role of NGOs in the country.

Another form of negation is to define precisely what is *legitimate* voluntary action. Some attempts have been made in this regard, under the guise of developing appropriate criteria and guidelines for providing government funding through various agencies and programmes. In the Seventh Plan Document chapter on voluntary agencies, a series of criteria for defining voluntary agencies and the role that they play in rural poverty-alleviation programmes are listed. This tends to legitimize only that which has been mentioned in the Plan document. Anything other than that is considered illegitimate; thus, anything outside the officially provided definition can be construed as illegitimate. In public forums, party leaders and government officials have begun to prescribe roles for voluntary agencies. In a recent public meeting in Rajasthan, a senior minister and a senior official proposed that voluntary agencies should engage in constructive work, and not in educating and organizing the people.

The third response of the state is even more sophisticated and complex. It entails co-option, a subtle mechanism for neutralizing the voluntary agency and its leadership. Co-option by the state takes several forms: providing funds is an easy method as, once a voluntary agency becomes dependent on government funds for its ongoing programmes and survival, then the state quietly enters into the agency and neutralizes its potential for effective contribution. KVIC[7] is the classic example of this. Enough evidence exists to suggest that funding a voluntary agency has been the state's most potent neutralizing tool. The second form of co-option is the incorporation of voluntary-agency leaders into state bodies and committees. Voluntary agencies are made a party to certain decisions, but the state goes ahead and implements them the way its machinery permits. Leaders of voluntary agencies feel bound, with "one leg in" the state. Many NGO leaders have spent more than half their time in the past two or three years in state capitals and Delhi attending such meetings and events, thereby away from the field. This is not to suggest that voluntary agencies should not influence state policies and programmes. They should. But it is important to keep in view the potential pitfalls and digressions of this path, particularly since many leaders of voluntary agencies become enamoured by the "recognition" bestowed upon them by the state.

In this context, reference needs to be made to the recent trend of finding sensitive and sympathetic senior-government officials. At such high levels (particularly in central government) many sensitive, positive and sympathetic officials have begun to espouse the cause of voluntary agencies. This trend need not be confused with any significant changes in the character of the state. A few

sensitive officials are only a small part of the state apparatus, and blind faith in their ability to ensure continued
support for voluntary agencies needs to be questioned.

The weaknesses of voluntary agencies

The response of the state in the face of opposition created
by voluntary agencies is aimed at domesticating, neutralizing, regulating and controlling them. In a way, the state
in India is becoming increasingly successful in doing this,
particularly due to certain internal weaknesses that exist
within voluntary agencies.

The first set of weaknesses relate to a growing lack of
inner strength and faith in voluntarism and the meaning
of their work. If a voluntary agency does not value its own
work, if it is not able to situate its work within a larger
historical and socio-political framework, if its leaders and
members do not have inner strength and conviction about
their potential contribution, if they lack commitment to the
spirit of voluntarism and the causes for which they work,
then it is easy for the state and its agents to negate their
value. Many voluntary agencies are suffering from this.

The second set of weaknesses relates to the limited
understanding of the state and its character on the one
hand, and the dynamics of the voluntary agency and its
leadership on the other. As a voluntary agency becomes
established, as its work spreads and its staff expands, as
it becomes a stable organizational entity, pressures for
maintaining the status quo increase. As the founder-
leaders of a voluntary agency mature, get established in
life, have a growing family, and approach middle age,
questions emerge like "Who am I?", "What have I contri-
buted?", "Has my sacrifice been worth it?". The life-cycle
of a voluntary agency, and the life-cycle of its founder-
leader(s) interact to create situations where recognition
from the state becomes an important goal, and is sought

and pursued, openly or not. It is in such circumstances that co-option by the state becomes relatively easy.

Finally, internal weakness relating to a lack of adequate systems, procedures, financial and programme-control measures, tend to provide fuel for attack and harassment from the state. Once attacked, a voluntary agency finds itself alone, isolated and weak. In our quest for autonomy and independence, in our drive to be flexible, self-reliant and self-sufficient, voluntary agencies and their leaders today remain divided, unorganized and isolated. We are separated by caste, ideology, region, language, nature of work, type of funding, and so on. We have no mechanism of mutual support and solidarity; we have not shown our collective strength in support of each others' well-being and survival. Hence, attacks on and the harassment of individual voluntary agencies by the state continue unchallenged and unquestioned. The state and its agents know this weakness of ours. Do we?

Where has voluntarism gone?

It is in this overall context that we need to look at the relationship between *voluntarism* and *state-ism*. In India, there has been a growing trend towards state-ism over the last 30 to 40 years. The state has begun to play an all-pervasive, all-present, all-dominating, all resource-controlling developmental role; the state is everywhere in India. It is in health, education, agriculture, rural development, women's programmes, environment, pollution, ecology, forestry, and even the "organization of the beneficiaries". In contrast to state-ism, the spirit of voluntarism implies freedom and democracy. Voluntarism represents the spirit of freedom, and the free association of thoughts and action. Voluntarism is equivalent to democracy and democratic functioning; it implies that there is the socio-political space for pluralism, diversity and complexity.

In the last 30 years, with the growing role of the state and state-ism in India, there is a shrinking of space for voluntarism and voluntary action. Historically, fascism and authoritarian forces have gained strength whenever there has been such a weakening. So, in order to preserve, sustain and strengthen democracy, we need to strengthen voluntarism and voluntary action. We need to *recover the essential meaning of voluntarism* and voluntary action in our country. We need to rediscover the meaning of the people's own control, own action, own vision, own dreams, own experience as essential ingredients in changing and improving their life situation, and not continuing to depend on the state and state-ism. Unless we can change the terms of this discourse, unless we can redefine the meaning inherent in the concept of voluntarism, unless we can recover the essential spirit of voluntarism for our people, we will not be able to enlarge the space needed for its continued growth, nurture and strength.

It is in this context that the nature of the relationship between governmental and non-governmental organizations has to be viewed: the context of the roles that NGOs play, the meaning of these roles *vis-à-vis* the state and its agents, the history of NGOs in a given socio-political framework, and the response of the state to the roles played by the NGOs. Without such a historical and specific analysis, without situating this analysis within the overall meaning and appreciation of the spirit of voluntarism and its equivalence to democracy, any attempt at collaboration between non-governmental and governmental organizations would get bogged down by a narrow and only partial understanding of such mechanisms. It is important that we recognize the crucially inherent and essential meaning of voluntarism as the expression of human freedom, human spirit, as liberation from bondage, as resistance to control, as protest against oppression. Only then we will be able to come to grips with the contradictions inherent in the relationship of voluntary agencies and the state.

NOTES

1. The lower castes in the Hindu social system, which were "scheduled" for preferential treatment, or affirmative action, by the Indian government.
2. "Tribals" refers to the aboriginals of India who live in traditional societies based on the collective ownership of resources. They presently constitute 7 per cent of the population.
3. CAPART (the Council for the Advancement of Peoples' Action and Rural Technology) is an autonomous organization created by the government of India to channel funds to voluntary agencies involved in rural development and the promotion of rural technology.
4. Patwaries are the lowest level revenue officers in an Indian village, who keep land records and collect land revenue.
5. BDOs are Block Development Officers and are in charge of all development programmes at block level (the level below district).
6. DWCRA stands for the Development of Women and Children in Rural Areas, a programme of the government of India's Ministry of Rural Development, to promote income-generating programmes for poor women through women's collective efforts.
7. KVIC is a semi-autonomous government body created to channel funds and create marketing networks for Khadi and Village Industries at a local level.

2. Ten Years of Experience with Participatory Action Research in South Asia – Lessons for NGOs and Peoples' Organizations

by Ponna Wignaraja

Ponna Wignaraja is the Chairperson of the Participatory Institute for Development Alternatives (PIDA) in Sri Lanka; he has also been the Secretary General of the Society for International Development (SID) and Head of the South Asian section of the United Nations University's Asian Perspectives Project from which this paper is derived. During his time at SID, Ponna Wignaraja started the Grass Roots Initiatives and Strategies Programme (GRIS) which has been a valuable forum for the discussion of the possible participation by the poor in development programmes. This chapter is a summary by Janet Durno of a longer piece by Ponna Wignaraja.

Against the background of the failure of over 25 years of development efforts in South Asia to benefit the poor, two specific initiatives emerged in the mid 1970s. South Asian organizations (particularly in India and Bangladesh) began to experiment with alternative ways of raising the awareness of the rural poor and mobilizing them to undertake self-reliant actions and improve their livelihood. In addition, a group of concerned social scientists, reflecting upon the failure of past development efforts, began to interact with the emerging grassroots initiatives that were undertaking the analysis, conceptualization and development of new perspectives and methodologies.

Social Structure and Explanations

Source: Richard Holloway and David Watson (eds), *Changing Focus – Involving the Rural Poor in Development Planning* (Oxford and IBH Publishing: New Delhi, 1989).

Three of these pioneering grassroots programmes were
the Rural Action Project in India (later an NGO called the
People's Institute for Development and Training, PIDT);
PROSHIKA in Bangladesh; and a government action
research programme in Sri Lanka that eventually also
became an NGO called the Participatory Institute for
Development Alternatives (PIDA). By 1982, not only had
these experimental programmes increased their action
research activities, but many more such initiatives had
emerged in other South Asian countries (and, indeed, in
other countries in the world).

From the experience of the last 10 years, three clear
lessons have emerged for NGOs and people's organizations committed to reversing dominant processes, building
new power structures, and exerting vigilance over
community-development programmes as they relate to
internal and external forces for change. The lessons were
that it was important:

  (i) to continue sustained analysis and conceptualization,
      not only to demystify and criticize conventional
      development thinking and the new orthodoxies in
      development theories and "solutions", but also to
      cohere positive new approaches based on experi-
      ments in participatory self-reliant development;

 (ii) to continue to experiment with the methodology of
      Participatory Action Research (PAR) as part of the
      people's "praxis" in overcoming their own prob-
      lems and evolving a methodology by which the gap
      between knowledge and action, between develop-
      ment and under-development in poor countries can
      be bridged; *and*

(iii) to sensitize (and train) cadres of "second-generation"
      activists/researchers in each country, who will have
      the capacity and skills to take up the challenge of
      applying participatory self-reliant development on a

broader basis by undertaking new experiments and initiatives.

This paper is chiefly concerned with the first two of the above points.

Elements for further conceptualization

Following the Second World War, most Third World countries emerged from colonialism as politically independent nations. They tended to adopt a development model which, in the context of the present discussion, had two important characteristics:

(i) the process of "development" envisaged by the model was so structured at the macro level that it allowed the continuation of existing international economic relationships; *and*

(ii) the model was unspecific at the operational level. It did not ask what kind of institutions would be required locally in order to implement the macro objectives or how the existing political, social and cultural institutions would react to the growth process envisaged by the macro model.

A basic premise of the old framework of development was that there was one stock of knowledge (i.e., modern technology) located in industrialized countries which, if transferred to the Third World, would solve most of its problems. Today, however, it has become clear that not only is this technology in many ways creating impoverishment (as well as being a carrier of often undesirable cultural codes and values), but also that it is only one of a variety of technological choices open to the Third World. Traditional, intermediate and newly created technologies are other, and perhaps much more valid, possibilities. The strategy of technological choice can no longer be left solely to the technocrats but must be related to a social philosophy, the local resource position and factor distribution.

A second element that needs to be demystified is the "project approach" which, despite the fact that experience has shown its limitations (particularly in rural situations), remains deeply rooted in the current operations of most governments, donor agencies and so-called integrated rural development programmes. The interdependence and connections between different village activities seriously limit the potential of the project approach, which assumes that there is a beginning and a defined end to "the project", and that the inputs and outputs are quantifiable. Too often, projects are forced into a preconceived technical plan designed from the top, without the involvement and understanding of the target group. Conventional cost-benefit analysis theory is also inadequate in designing or developing activities in a situation in which there is a lack of access to resources and a need to minimize waste.

Technocratically evolved project packages tend to polarize the village; the rich inhabitants get richer while the poor get poorer. Even when a package is aimed at a "target" group identified as the rural poor, and is carried out with some attempt at consultation with them (an act which is often confused with participation), it does not in itself ensure that the economic benefits will reach the poor, let alone improve their condition in wider human terms. Projects must evolve from the needs and perceptions of the groups at which they are aimed and be built upon the collective experience of previous attempts at development. This can lead to a self-reliant base, into which external technical and financial inputs can be absorbed without the benefits being channelled towards the already well-off.

A last point that needs clarifying is one related to the concept of the homogeneous community, that is the "harmony" situation. Rural communities in the Third World are not homogeneous entities. In most Third World villages, there are sharp contradictions among different groups with conflicting interests. Dominance–dependency relationships give the wealthier class the power to threaten the immediate survival of the poor. For example, the poor tenant may be dependent on the landlord not just for the possession of land, but also for credit, tubewell[1] water, equipment rental and transport for carrying produce to market. It can no longer be disputed that as long as the basic economic and social institutions in the village are controlled by the rich, merely assisting the poor *per se* will not safeguard them against the manipulations of those in power.

Any strategy of rural development involving the poor and oppressed has to begin by uniting them. Due to deep-rooted dependency relationships and inequality, the poor lack unity and have become "non-innovative" and "non-experimental". Under these circumstances, dependency on the rich must be reduced in order to give the poor independent staying power in a conflict-ridden social environment, and to enable them to benefit from development efforts. A meaningful approach to development must therefore be a political approach. In some cases, the "political space" already exists for such an approach. In others, it must be created.

Not all the poor societies of South Asia are in the same stage of historical development. Having been incorporated (along with other Third World countries) into a global system over which they have little control, these societies have not made a meaningful transition either to capitalism or socialism, nor have they been able to eradicate the worst levels of poverty and hunger. Poor villagers have a growing sense of alienation and are concerned about the waste of resources and the value of the available knowledge base. The many contradictions that are apparent are resulting in political and social unrest, and growing militarism which could lead to revolutionary changes or to complete de-stabilization and the breakdown of society.

There is still very little understanding of the interactions between the internal developments of a country and external geo-political constellations, or among the forces that are heightening micro-level contradictions. Third World scientists have attempted to analyse development processes from two perspectives. The first line of research has been organized around the Latin American Dependency[2] and the African Centre-Periphery[3] theses. The second line of research, still in its infancy, criticizes a predetermined universalism and stresses pluralism, including geo-cultural specificity. The basic premise is that development is simultaneously a "top-down" and a "bottom-up" process, that is a process of human development, of social transformation in which people are both the subject and the object and in which they participate at all levels of decision-making. The new style of research, though giving some space to micro–macro interconnections is primarily concerned with the set of problems centred around the grass-roots micro level. It squarely faces the issues of participation, awareness raising and the building of people's power as part of an on-going social process – the long revolution towards social and structural transition and change in Asia.

The experience of developing countries in both the capitalist and socialist frameworks indicates the need consciously to create grassroots institutions through which the people can act against the systematic tendency towards dependence and inequity (as in peripheral capitalist economies), and the tendency towards centralization and bureaucracy (as in planned economies). In a situation where the local state apparatus is not uniformly strong, the nexus of contradictions between oppressor and oppressed may provide considerable space for the oppressed to develop locally effective power structures and organizations. For example, the poor peasants of one particular village may have access to unused and dispersed resources which, through co-operative effort and the use of up-graded indigenous technology, could provide them with resources (such as land, fertilizer and water) that they may individually lack. Similarly, organized pressure by the poor upon the local administration or landlords can force them to concede to cheaper credit, better health facilities and lower rent rates. If scattered grassroots organizations were able to sustain each other through an ongoing exchange of ideas, they could contribute to the eventual emergence not just of a new consciousness, but also of a new kind of structure in which decentralized power and mass participation in economic/social decision-making could be a real possibility. This is where participatory development may have immediate relevance and far-reaching implications for the future shape of society in Asia and other Third World countries.

Salient features of the new methodology of PAR

The starting point of the new methodology of participatory action research (PAR) is to view development in funda-mental humanistic terms as a process of bringing out the creative potential of the people, in particular the poor and oppressed. Self-reliance and participation are the corner-stones of the development process. In view of the contra-dictions inherent in Asian rural communities, it is essential that the poor investigate, analyse and understand the socio-economic realities of their environment, in particular the forces which create their poverty and oppression. This understanding would give them the ability and confidence to change reality through collective action.

It is difficult, however, for such a self-reliant process to take place spontaneously. In the context of attitudes of dependency and lack of unity, a catalytic intervention by an action researcher or agent of change is usually a necessary initial input. Such agents of change identify with the rural poor, mobilize them, raise their awareness and help them to organize for participatory self-reliant development.

PAR is a methodology for social mobilization and awareness which involves socio-political action and research in order to produce scientific knowledge *with* and *for* the people and people's groups. It is a process of sensitization; of learning by exposure to concrete village situations; of investigation and the analysis of the realities of village life; of sharing and comparing experiences in the action/reflection process of "praxis". Its final aim is to build people's power and to enhance life.

PAR is characterized by several important features:

(i) catalytic initiatives taken by action researchers (e.g., concerned academics) resulting in an interaction between two ways of life and traditions; that is, the community (involved in the original struggle for survival, with their practical and down-to-earth traditions) and the researcher (coming more from the formal intellectual tradition but aware of and committed to people's goals).

(ii) Through this interaction, the poor/oppressed are stimulated to carry out their own investigation and analysis of the reality in which they live, thereby promoting critical awareness of the socio-economic environment. The creative tension that arises out of this interaction has the potential for change.

(iii) As it unfolds, the process is characterized by a critical recovery of people's historical traditions, the re-evaluation of their culture, and the re-establishment of people's dignity and strength. Their creativity is released.

(iv) The critical awareness of their reality leads people to undertake organized collective action in order to change this reality in their favour, thereby improving their socio-economic status according to their own self-determined priorities, primarily using their own resources, initiatives and skills.

(v) A process of people's "praxis" (i.e., a progressive action/reflection rhythm) is set in motion. People's own cadres and catalytic skills emerge out of the praxis, thereby at least partially replacing the role earlier played by the external researcher.

(vi) The process cannot thrive in isolation as a micro phenomenon. There is a need for linkage and multiplication without which the process cannot be a transformational one leading to social change. PAR is a continuous process without a time limit; it is an open model which cannot be pre-planned.

(vii) The process results in new knowledge derived from the partnership between the researcher and the people in a subject-to-subject framework. The breaking up of the exploitative subject (researcher) to object (people) relationship offers a new opportunity for creativity and the production of greater knowledge about life experiences.

PAR is a collective research effort aimed at retrieving knowledge about the living reality of the people; their own perceptions of history, culture and traditions (as distinct from the versions of the élite; and the people's priorities and needs. The knowledge so generated has inherent value and thus the structural separation between knowledge and action, between experts and people, is dissolved. It is a knowledge which belongs to the people and which must be returned to them for the enhancement of their lives.

As PAR is a pioneer methodology which is still evolving, there is a need for further experimentation and conceptualization in order to establish its viability as an alternative to existing social knowledge and development action. One central issue is the validity of the PAR process (which is evolved from micro-situations) at the macro level, and its ability to come to terms with the issues of handling state power, of choosing a revolutionary class to work with, and selecting appropriate organizational forms. There is, however, a growing body of evidence which suggests that the praxis generated by the PAR methodology, by establishing a new relationship between intellectuals and agents of change in the field, is providing a new agenda for politics in many Asian countries. As formal institutions weaken and decline, and élitist state structures lose contact with the majority of the poor, it is the grassroots PAR organizations which are providing an institutional basis for those people marginalized by conventional development processes, enabling them not only to survive but also to develop on their own terms.

NOTES
1. A shallow borehole with a manual or motor-driven pump, used as a well for water for irrigation.
2. The well-known theory that explains the under-development of Latin America as being due to historical and current economic connections with and dependency upon once colonial and now neo-colonial powers.
3. The theory describing development in African countries of a single capital city which responds to the needs of the modern sector and "colonizes" the rural areas, drawing off the surplus and forcing the rural areas to provide the level of production that the modern sector needs.

3.   Siro Mallik Goes to Buy a Pair of Bullocks and a Cart

by Joe Madiath

Joe Madiath is the Director of Gram Vikas, an Indian NGO working with tribals in Orissa State. It has been particularly successful in social forestry projects. This is an abridged version of an article originally written for the *Indian Express*.

Siro Mallik is a 48-year-old Khond tribal, living in Tamana village, situated in the foot hills of the Kerandimal range of hills. The village is connected to the main road by a dirt track. Siro had two acres of land, 28 mango trees, six tamarind trees and two Jack fruit trees. Of the two acres, he mortgaged one nine years ago to a landlord for 300 rupees, to meet the expenses of the marriage of his daughter, Tulsa. The mortgage agreement was that the landlord would release the land only after 10 years, after paying the capital with 60 per cent compound interest and, for the 10 years, the landlord would cultivate the land. If after 10 years Siro was not able to repay the capital and interest, the land would belong to the landlord.

Eight years ago Siro lost his old father. He was ailing for quite sometime and Siro had spent a lot of money on quack doctors and on black magic. On the death of his father, Siro had to feed his village and relations. He had no money. He approached the same money-lender for 500 rupees. The latter gave him the money most willingly, but on his terms. Siro had to mortgage his remaining one acre

Gaps between Government and the Villagers' Perceptions

*". . . perhaps you don't know that we've electrified
your villages, given you better water supply, roads,
schools, hospitals . . ."*

Source: Cartoon by R.K. Laxman in *New Internationalist*, September 1984;
originally published in *The Times of India*.

of land for six years, on the same terms and conditions as
before.

Seven years ago Siro had a serious attack of typhoid. He
could not go to the jungle to cut firewood. His wife also
could not go to the jungle as she had to look after Siro.
There was no money in the house. Siro Mallik's wife

approached a money-lender. He gave her 80 rupees for the six tamarind and two Jack fruit trees. The money-lender had full rights to the fruits of these eight trees for the next 25 years. After 25 years, if Siro returned the capital with the interest of 60 per cent, the trees would be returned to him.

As Siro was sick and he had lost his land, he could not repair and thatch his house. In a pre-monsoon storm, the roof of his house was blown away. Siro approached the village *Shundi*, or liquor merchant, for 120 rupees, who gave him the money readily in exchange for the mortgage of 20 of Siro's best mango trees. These could be redeemed after a period of 15 years, after paying the interest and capital.

Siro was impoverished systematically. He lost his initiative to work to save. He had lost all hopes of getting back any of his property.

Five years ago, the Khond tribals of the Kerandimals came together. They formed their own organization called "Kerandimal Gana Sanghatan (KGS)".[1] Together with Gram Vikas, a voluntary organization which began working six years ago in the Kerandimals and which had initiated the organization of the Kerandimal tribals, KGS began systematically to build their organization. People had been made aware of the recently passed law of moratorium on rural indebtedness. The people realized how exploited they were by the landlords, money-lenders and liquor merchants. Getting back all tribal property became a focal point of the tribals' organization.

Through a long drawn out struggle, Siro Mallik got back his land and trees. He was a happy man. He wanted to cultivate his land. He had no bullocks. So he decided to take a loan from a bank to buy a pair of bullocks. To make optimum use of the bullocks, he decided also to purchase a bullock cart. He knew that the commercial banks give loans for the purchase of bullocks and carts. He also knew that there was a bank established at Mohuda in the Gram Vikas campus, mainly to cater to the needs of the tribals. Siro went to the bank manager. He had to wait till 11.30 in the morning for the bank to open. He met the manager and told him of his need.

The bank manager said: "I cannot do anything directly. You go to the BDO [Block Development Officer] and let him recommend your case. Then we will give you the loan."

The next day Siro went to the office of the BDO, which is 20 kilometres away. He had to walk all the way. On reaching there, he found to his dismay that the BDO was out of headquarters. Nobody could tell him when the BDO would be available. So he trekked painfully back to Tamana. He had to go four more times before he could meet the BDO.

"Why did you come to me?" the BDO said when he ultimately met him. "I cannot know everyone in a Block. You go to your Gram Sevak, let him identify you and let him certify that you are a tribal. Then we will recommend your case to the bank."

Siro began his hunt for the Gram Sevak, who is now the VAW (Village Agricultural Worker). The VAWs are implementing World Bank financed agricultural extension programmes, where they are to implement the T & V (Training and Visit) method. But T & V as it is practised today stands for "Touch and Vanish". Siro had to make seven "pilgrimages" to the house of the VAW, who stays in the town, before he could meet him. The VAW asked Siro to meet him in the evening of the next day.

Siro went the next day to the VAW, where upon the VAW said to Siro, "On the strength of my certificate you will get a fifty per cent subsidy for the loan from the government. You know that one has to incur certain expenses to get a certificate like this. But why should you bother? You are getting a fifty per cent subsidy. So you can be generous with a VAW."

As a gesture of generosity, 25 rupees passed hands before he got an Identification Certificate.

Siro took the hard won certificate to the BDO, again meeting him after three visits.

"No this won't do," said the BDO. "This certificate has to be countersigned by the AEO [Agricultural Extension Officer]."

Siro went four times to the office of the AEO, but the AEO could not be found in his office. Hence, Siro went thrice to his house and ultimately met him.

"No, you have to come to the office, why do you come to my residence?"

"Sir," Siro said apologetically, "I have gone several times to your office to meet you, but I could not find you."

"Yes," said the AEO, "I am a busy man. Most of the time I am out on tour. Anyway, you come the next Monday and meet me in the office."

Siro went on the specified Monday, met the AEO and got the certificate countersigned.

Siro thought that he was at the end of the road to getting the bullocks, as he approached the BDO's office with the certificate signed by the VAW and countersigned by the AEO. He rejoiced all the more because even the BDO was present in the office this time.

"Aagaya," Siro addressed the BDO with the Oriya equivalent of Sir. "I have got the certificate countersigned by AEO Babu."

"Very good, let me see it," the BDO said. Siro very proudly produced the fruit of his painful tracks.

The BDO looked at the certificate very intensely, then pronounced the verdict: "This is good, but it is not enough. You have to get a Feasibility Certificate from the VAS [Veterinary Assistant Surgeon]. The VAS has to certify that you have the necessary facilities to keep a pair of bullocks.''

Siro's head began to reel. He caught the chair in front to steady himself. After a few moments, he managed to ask:

''Aagaya, what feasibility study is required for the keeping of bullocks by a farmer?''

The BDO was not in a mood to explain. ''How can you,'' he asked imperiously, ''ask such a question? These are government rules and you have to follow them if you want to get the loan and the subsidy. Besides, the people who made these rules are more learned than you and they know what they were doing.''

Siro could only say ''Aagaya,'' fold his hands in a reverent gesture of *namaskar*, and go out of the BDO's office.

Siro felt tired and sick and wished that he had never started on this trail of acquiring a pair of bullocks. A lesser mortal would have given up, but he pulled himself together and went to the veterinary dispensary nearby. The VAS was not present. The attendant told him that if he came in the morning the next day, he could meet him.

Siro faithfully came the next morning to the veterinary dispensary, trekking 20 kilometres into the bargain. He met the VAS, explained his predicament, and requested a Feasibility Certificate.

''How can I,'' asked the VAS self-righteously, ''give you a certificate, without visiting your house and ascertaining the feasibility for myself? I do not have the time in the near future to visit you as your village is quite far, and besides the road is very bad even for my motorcycle. You know that the government does not give me any TA [travel allowance] for such a visit, so you will have to pay for the fuel.''

''Aagaya, how much?'' asked Siro.

''Fifty rupees. But why should you worry, you are a tribal and you are getting a fifty per cent subsidy.''

"Aagaya, fifty rupees is too much for a poor tribal like me to pay."

"If you want the certificate it will cost you that much. Petrol is not cheap these days."

"I will pay the fifty rupees."

"Achaa!! Have you the fifty rupees with you?"

"No Sir, I will bring it tomorrow."

"I will give the certificate tomorrow."

"What about your visit?"

"It won't be necessary. I will give you a Feasibility Certificate without visiting your village. But, remember to bring fifty rupees when you come tomorrow."

"Aagaya."

Siro went home, a completely dejected man. In the evening he got 50 rupees – at 72 per cent interest. The next day he went to the VAS, handed over the fifty rupees and got the certificate. Thereafter he went to the BDO and showed him all the certificates.

The BDO scrutinized the documents and pronounced: "Since you are getting a pair of bullocks and bullock cart, you have to get another Feasibility Certificate from the IPO [Industrial Promotion Officer], because a bullock cart comes within the purview of Industry."

Siro's feelings can only be imagined. He walked out of the BDO's office without even the customary *namaskar*.

Siro went eight times to the District Industries Centre to meet the IPO, who, he was told, was always on tour. Ultimately he tracked him down to his residence.

The IPO came straight to the point. "You will have to pay me twenty-five rupees and I will give you the certificate. After all, how does it matter to you, you are getting a fifty per cent subsidy."

"Aagaya, I am a poor man. How can I pay twenty-five rupees?"

"You see, I am not asking all the twenty-five rupees for myself. I have to give a major portion to the office. When any dignatory or officer comes on visit or inspection, we have to entertain him. If I don't take anything from you, how can I meet all these expenses? From my salary? So you come tomorrow at ten o'clock to my office with the money and I will give you the certificate."

Siro went to the IPO's office the next day at the appointed time with twenty-five rupees borrowed from the same money-lender at 72 per cent interest. He handed the money over to the IPO and got the Feasibility Certificate in exchange.

From the IPO's office, Siro went to the office of the BDO – a distance of 10 kilometres. The BDO was absent. The next day he went again and handed over his loan application with all the certificates to the BDO who said:

"You go to your village. Now I will officially forward your application to the bank. It will be there within a week's time."

Siro waited for a week and enquired at the bank as to whether his application had been forwarded by the BDO. The answer was no. Siro went to the BDO again, who said, "I have not forwarded your application yet, because I was waiting for a few more applications, so that I could send them all together to the bank."

"Aagaya, I am after this loan for the last four months. How many times I have come to your office? God alone knows the trouble I went through. Please forward my application to the bank."

"OK. I will forward it today."

After a week the bank received the "duly forwarded application". Siro met the manager, who told him: "I have got the application from the BDO with the certificates. However, there are still two certificates you should obtain. Besides our bank there is the Co-operative Bank and the Land Mortgage Bank working in this area. Go and get from the two banks their NDCs [No Due Certificates]."

"Aagaya, I have not taken any loans from any bank. Please believe me and give me the loan."

"How can I believe you? I cannot give you the loan without their certificates."

Siro went to the Secretary of the Primary Co-operative Society and requested the No Due Certificate.

"It will cost you ten rupees."

"I thought it was free."

"Nothing is free, my dear man," the secretary chirped in wisely, "and why should you grudge giving me a petty ten rupees, when you are getting a fifty per cent subsidy?"

Siro parted with ten rupees in exchange for the No Due Certificate from the Primary Co-operative Society.

Next he had to contact the Area Supervisor of the Land Mortgage Bank. It was a very difficult job, contacting him. After five visits to the office, he found out his residence in the town and went there one day early in the morning and requested the certificate.

"I will verify records to see if you have any dues. You come and meet me in the office after three days and I will see if I can give you the No Due Certificate."

"Aagaya, I have gone to your office not less than five times and I could not find you so I came today to your house. You know very well that not only I but none from our village has ever got any loan from your bank."

"In that case I will give you a certificate and save you any further trouble, but it will cost you twenty rupees."

Siro gave him 20 rupees the next day, and got the No Due Certificate.

Siro went to the bank again and gave the bank manager all the papers. After scrutinizing the papers the manager said: "The papers seems to be in order. Now you can get a thousand rupees for the bullocks." Siro forgot for the moment all the agony he had gone through and enquired, "Will you give me the money today? I have seen a good pair of bullocks for a thousand rupees. If you give the money to me I shall buy them tomorrow."

"No, the money cannot be given to you. There is a Purchasing Committee comprising of the BDO or his representative, the VAS, the IPO and my Field Officer and myself. We will go to Kanchili Animal Hat (market) next Sunday and purchase a pair of bullocks for you."

"Aagaya, I know best what sort of bullocks are best suited for me and I would prefer to buy a local pair. So please give me the money."

"No, that cannot be done. The bullocks have to be purchased by experts and, besides, if I give you the money, you might even misuse it. We want to ensure that you buy a pair of good bullocks."

Siro was aghast. But he could do very little to change the course of events.

The next Sunday was not suitable for the members of the Purchasing Committee and hence the Sunday after that was fixed. The members of the Purchasing Committee got into a Jeep and Siro sat at the back of the Jeep on the floor.

As the Jeep arrived at the market, the sellers knew that bank people had come to purchase animals. The dress of the Purchasing Committee distinguished them from the rest of the farmers. Immediately the price of the animals shot up. The Committee members got rather vexed after a few bargains and at the end decided on a pair of bullocks for 1,200 rupees (the Committee having decided that a further loan of 200 rupees should be granted to Siro). Siro was not happy with the selected animals.

"These are rather old bullocks, they will not last more than two seasons. Such a pair I could get in my locality for less than seven hundred rupees. Please do not purchase them and give me just a thousand rupees, and I will buy the type of bullocks I want."

The Purchasing Committee would hear nothing of this.

They bought the pair of bullocks and handed them over to Siro, sat in the Jeep and sped away.

Siro, instead of being jubilant, was a very unhappy man as he started his long trek with the bullocks back to the village. Little did Siro know that he would also have to meet the fuel expenses of the Jeep and other "associated expenses" that the Purchasing Committee had incurred. As he walked back he really had doubts whether the bank which gave him a loan at 12 per cent interest, and the government machinery which gave him a 50 per cent subsidy, were any less exploitative than the money-lender, who gave him money at 72 per cent interest, but without any delay or red tape.

Siro had to wait over four months to get the loan. He spent 48 days running after the different officials to get the different certificates. He had to show a "gesture of generosity" (more commonly known as a bribe) at almost every stage. He paid a total of 130 rupees as bribes. His lost wages, at eight rupees a day, amounted to 384 rupees. He had spent another 120 rupees on food and travel. Ultimately he got a pair of bullocks, which he didn't like and which cost him 1,200 rupees. Left to himself he could have secured them for a maximum of 700 rupees. His total loss was 1,134 rupees.

Siro approached the bank manager a few days later.

"Aagaya, when will I get my bullock cart?"

"For your bullock cart, you have to get quotations from at least three people who make these carts. These will be scrutinized by the IPO and our Field Officer and, if the price is OK, one of them will be approved. We will place an order and when it is ready you can collect it."

All the miles that he had to travel, the miles of red tape that he had to encounter, the bribes that he had to give at every stage, and the humiliations that he had to face flashed into Siro's mind. He did not hesitate to say:

"Aagaya, I do not need another loan and I do not want a bullock cart." He walked out.

Who benefited from the bank loan? Who benefited from the subsidy? How will Siro repay the money-lender? How will Siro repay the bank loan? If Siro becomes a defaulter in repayment of his loan, who is to blame? If the ordinary people do not have faith in the programme and projects of the government, can you blame them? While we answer or do not answer these questions, thousands of Siro's are going through this bureaucratic guillotine of apathy, corruption, indifference and total disregard every day.

NOTES
1. For details, see Joe Madiath, "Tribal resurgence in Ganjam" in *Voluntary Action*, July/August 1981; and Anthya Madiath, "When Tribal's awake: The Kerandimal movement" in Walter Fernandez (ed.), *People's Participation in Development* (Indian Social Institute: New Delhi).

4. Legal Rights for Poor Women – SLARTC in India

by Janet Durno and Manabendra Mandal

SLARTC stands for the Socio-Legal Aid Research and Training Centre in Calcutta, West Bengal, India. It has been working for many years to give the poor some knowledge of the law and their rights under the Indian Constitution. The piece by Janet Durno, written for CUSO, describes the work of the Women's Cell which specializes in the legal education of women. Janet Durno is a consultant for CUSO and the International Development Research Centre (IDRC) on development topics and spent some time visiting SLARTC's fieldwork in 1986. The piece by Manabendra Mandal, the Director of SLARTC, places the organization's work in the context of Indian law and government. It is an excerpt from the 1987 Annual Report.

Socio-Legal Aid and Training for People's Development

by Janet Durno

The sun set at the end of the dry field in a haze of dusty light and suddenly it was cool. It was almost the end of winter. Shipra wrapped a shawl around her shoulders, a yellow one, the colour of spring, and called at the next house for her friend. Together they walked into the village and joined the crowd waiting for the reading of the Gita to begin. Shipra laughed and chatted with the other girls,

The Government's View of the Poor – and Poor Women's View of Themselves

ALL POOR PEOPLE ARE JUST THE SAME

Many households are headed by poor women

- Only one person may be able to work
- It is difficult to both work and bring up children
- Low-level jobs – low-level wages

Source: Richard Holloway and David Watson (eds), *Changing Focus – Involving the Rural Poor in Development Planning* (Oxford and IBH Publishing: New Delhi, 1989).

occasionally joining in the singing of the sacred words, and then turning back to the animated huddle of friendly gossip.

Now it was very dark, the best time of the day for women to go and relieve themselves in the field, safe from the eyes of men. Shipra accompanied her friend out of the lamplight and over the hard earth to a cluster of banana trees. As they began to make their way back, two of the young men of the village strolled up and asked the girls to come and sing with them. Her friend refused and hurried on but Shipra, carefree in the musical dark air, agreed. Minutes later – alerted by a look, a gesture, a muffled laugh – she was suddenly afraid. The young men caught her as she turned to run, tied the loose end of her saree over her mouth, and pulled her behind the trees where several other men were waiting. She looked from face to familiar face for rescue. They were all men she knew, sons of the village, but their eyes were strange in the dim light. They began to taunt her: how could she be so proud when her husband had abandoned her and even her own family no longer valued her? They could do as they liked; who was there to take revenge? And then they began to do as they liked, one after the other. She fainted as the fourth one came down on her.

An older man from the village found Shipra as she wandered across the field, searching vaguely for her shawl, her blouse torn and her hair dishevelled. Terrified, she tried to run and fell, whimpering, as he pulled her to her feet. The man listened to her story as he took her home, and by morning the entire village had heard. With the crime now impossible to conceal, Shipra overcame her shyness and shame, and accused the men of rape. Arrested and then let out on bail, they immediately began to threaten Shipra and her family. Suddenly there were no customers at the small shop owned by Shipra's father and no visitors in the family's home. People avoided them on the streets. Shipra's assailants were brash young hoodlums and so, fearing for their own daughters and property, the other villagers ostracized her entire family.

The case has not yet come up for trial. It may be that a trial will never be held. The men have money and the support of the village, even if it is only a support accorded by fear. For Shipra's family, the costs of pursuing legal action (a lawyer, court fees, and travel to town for themselves and their witnesses) would be prohibitive, and they are afraid of incurring further violence.

Shipra's case is being investigated by the SLARTC, a Calcutta-based organization which provides legal aid for the poor, organizes socio-legal training courses, and is involved in community-development programmes throughout the northern and north-eastern states of India. The organization was founded in 1983 by its present Executive Director, Mr Manabendra Mandal, in an effort to ameliorate the present situation in which legal services are largely unavailable for the 50 per cent of Indian people who live on or below the poverty line, and who must daily face injustices without the possibility of redress. For these people, justice flees before the whim of a rich man or the fist of a thug.

The existing legal mechanisms are far-off towns which can only be reached on foot or in a crowded bus, the day's wages lost, and the expenses covered by a high-interest loan which places the whole future of the already debt-ridden villager in jeopardy. The situation is exacerbated by the people's ignorance of their basic legal rights and privileges, and the lack of solidarity among villagers and slum-dwellers divided by socio-economic status, caste, religion and sex. Ignorance and lack of unity leave the people vulnerable to exploitation and easy prey for land-owners, employers and local élites who twist and ignore the laws, frequently subverting government functions to serve their own ends.

Shipra was referred to SLARTC by women from a local voluntary group who had taken one of the socio-legal courses offered by the organization. These courses, lasting eight to ten days, attempt to place the power of knowledge into the people's hands by providing social and rural development workers with information on Indian law, legal rights, and the social problems faced by underprivileged groups such as unwed mothers, widows and children. The social workers then transfer this knowledge to the local people through the formation of socio-legal cells in the villages. The members of these calls are themselves villagers. They work to increase public awareness of basic legal rights, and encourage other villagers to bring their problems to the legal cell for advice and help in mediation. Whenever possible, problems are solved at the village level without recourse to the expensive and lengthy procedures of the courts. Difficult cases, however, are referred to SLARTC which deals with the legal paperwork, negotiates with the police, and can call upon a network of 200 lawyers to give advice and handle court cases where necessary.

The legal problems faced by men revolve around land; those of women, around men. While SLARTC works with both men and women, it is women that are the main target group as they face the double burden of poverty and the oppression of a patriarchal society – an oppression sanctioned by custom, religion and in some cases by law. The Indian Constitution and the laws of the country have, at least in theory, improved the status of women to some extent but, in practice, the laws are often ignored and some of them actually encourage discrimination against women.

A number of civil laws vary depending on the religious faith of those involved. Since 1955, for example, a Hindu man has been allowed only one wife at a time while a Muslim man can contract up to four legal marriages. There is also a growing controversy over the allocation of responsibility for the support of a divorced woman. Section 125 of the Criminal Procedure Code states that all divorced women, irrespective of their community, are entitled to maintenance from the husband, but conservative Muslim leaders claim that Section 125 contravenes orthodox Muslim law and that divorced women should be maintained by their fathers or brothers or, failing this, by the State Wakf Boards.

The issue of maintenance is extremely important in India where poor women are often incapable of providing a decent living standard for themselves and their children due to lack of education and skills; and where parents are frequently unwilling or financially unable to take back a divorced daughter. Muslim women are especially vulnerable due to the ease and frequency of divorce in their community. Nevertheless, despite protests from women's groups, a number of more liberal Muslim leaders, and the opposition parties, the government is currently debating a bill that would exempt Muslim women from coverage under Section 125; they seem to be currently more concerned with appeasing fundamentalist Muslim voters than with ensuring equal rights for all Indian women.

The mere existence of a law does not, of course, ensure its enforcement. A divorced woman may not receive the maintenance she is legally entitled to; her ex-husband may support her for a few months and then cease to keep up the payments, necessitating a return to court that the woman can ill afford. Most women eventually give up the alimony struggle, and try to make their own livings as best they can.

Between August 1983 and June 1984, 188 women died in Delhi from burns. Some of the deaths were accidental, but many were suicides and murders. In the same period there were 90 female suicides and eight deaths from severe beating (see Raka Sinha, "No life to call her own", *The Statesman*, 2 March 1986). In the joint family system the new bride is an outsider, often victimized by her mother- and sisters-in-law in retaliation for their own life-long subjugation by the male members of the family. The bride is considered to be the property of her husband and receives little sympathy, even from her own family, if she is abused. While a divorced Hindu wife is entitled to

receive maintenance from her ex-husband until her remarriage, a dead wife frees the husband to marry again and
obtain another dowry. In extreme cases wives are mur-
dered, or beaten, tortured and harassed into suicide if they
do not bring enough dowry to the marriage or if their
parents do not accede to demands for further gifts. The
giving and taking of dowries has been illegal since the
Dowry Restriction Act of 1961, but, for most women, an
adequate dowry still remains a precondition for obtaining
a suitable bridegroom.

Deepti had been beaten regularly by her policeman
husband since their marriage, but her parents refused to
shelter her. After the birth of a daughter, the abuse
increased and her parents-in-law began demanding more
dowry, complaining that Deepti had not produced a son.
Her husband dared her to commit suicide and at one point
threatened her parents that he would kill her. Soon after
that, Deepti allegedly burned herself to death. The police
became suspicious of foul play when they discovered that
the soles of her feet were charred, indicating that Deepti
had been tied up and burned (in an accident or suicide,
the woman usually tries to run from the flames and the
feet remain unharmed). Deepti's brother has filed a suit
against the husband and SLARTC is providing legal
assistance.

This particular case is receiving a great deal of publicity
in the media, but each year hundreds of Indian wives
die in similar suspicious circumstances that are not
investigated. The accidents and suicides happen in the
home without witnesses and where it is easy to tamper
with the evidence. In addition, the public apathy towards
women's rights infects the police who often refuse to
register complaints or do not investigate properly; the
cases which are brought to trial may take months or years
to solve.

The situation is beginning to change as women's

organizations work to raise people's awareness, and as police and judges become more sympathetic. However, the vicious abuse of women is all too often condoned or ignored. The beatings and cruelty Deepti suffered before her death are the common lot of women, sanctioned by custom and accepted by families who urge daughters to stay with their husbands and submit. Lacking education, confidence and unity, women themselves help to perpetuate the myth that their sufferings are divinely ordained.

Deepti, like the majority of Indian women, was unaware of her rights under the law and lacked the support necessary for her to defy her in-laws' ill-treatment and illegal demands for more dowry. Women need not only to develop an awareness of their legal rights but also to understand the procedures of the law and the steps they can take to rectify an intolerable situation or to obtain redress for crimes committed against them. SLARTC's involvement in women's development grew out of the realization that the provision of legal aid to individual women helps only to solve immediate personal dilemmas and does little to challenge the underlying system of oppression and exploitation that continues to breed such problems. Nor does it encourage women to co-operate in protesting against injustices or in obtaining education, employment and basic rights. One woman on her own cannot defend herself; a group of village women, on the other hand, can quell a brutal husband or work together to earn the money which can free them from a fatal dependence on the earning power and uncertain generosity of their men.

Women require support and encouragement as they take their first steps on the unfamiliar road of self-assertion. SLARTC ran its first course on Women's Development from 27 October to 5 December 1984. Forty women social workers from Assam, Manipur, Orissa, West Bengal and Bangladesh attended. In 1985, a second course was held but had to be cut to three weeks due to insufficient funds. The courses included rural visits with two or three nights spent in the villages, and trips to women's institutions and groups, as well as lectures, case studies and group discussions.

Through SLARTC's Women's Development and Socio-Legal courses, emphasis is placed on developing women's organizations and groups; networking with other women's groups is also encouraged. SLARTC plans to develop a women's resource centre with dossiers on all the women's groups in the region, their areas of specialization, and the help they are prepared to offer in the form of training courses and information exchange. Through these groups, women's legal needs can be addressed, not as isolated cases, but rather within a framework of collective action for social change.

From Calcutta, the drive to Kolaghat (a town in the district of Midnapore) takes about two and a half hours. The land is flat and now, in February, it is empty and dry except for scattered vivid patches of new rice soaking in irrigated fields. The trees are dust-green and even the waterweeds seem withered in the ponds. A rook perches on a cow's tail, pecking beneath it – the only animated being under the afternoon sun.

Kolaghat stretches along the far bank of the wide brown Rupnarayan River. It consists of box-like shops patched together from mats and wood, selling sweets, utensils and repairs. The members of the Kolaghat women's group meet us with smiles and touches and laughter. Their sarees are bright as gardens; their gestures quick and vivacious. Bouquets of flowers are presented to Swagata and Mandira, the co-ordinators or SLARTC's women's programme, and also to me. The stems are bound together in a thick wand and the massed bunch of pink, purple and yellow asters, roses, bachelor buttons and snap-dragons is a child's dream of a bouquet. The women bring us water, soft drinks, coconuts and plates of sweets which sit and sit under a fly-dispersing fan wielded by one of the women until we finally persuade the group to share the sweets among them all.

This women's group was formed in 1984 when SLARTC held a socio-legal training course in the area and several of the women involved met to discuss the possibility of setting up an income-generating project. Some of them had taken a tailoring course two years previously, but had not known how to set up in business, and the sewing machine they had been given sat rusting in a back room. Women from the Self Help Handicrafts Society, a Calcutta women's co-operative, were called in to discuss the tailoring project. They helped the women of Kolaghat to amass a small amount of capital for purchasing thread and cloth, and arranged for them to receive orders through Self Help. The women decided to pool their earnings for the first three months to build up their society's fund, and new members are still required to contribute in this way. For women who need every penny they can earn, this was a difficult decision and emphasizes their commitment to the co-operative ideal.

There are now eight full-time members: four married, one divorced, one widowed, and two single. They work from 11 a.m. to 5.30 p.m., six days a week, sharing the three sewing machines which have been donated to them. They make pot-holders, tea cosies, cosmetic cases and baby clothes – some for export, some for local markets. Self Help has arranged for them to take a course in garment cutting and they have been receiving this instruction at the weekends for six weeks. The course should continue for another six weeks, but the trainer's husband, complaining of the "discomfort" he experiences at weekends when she is not at home to cook his food and prepare his tea, now refuses to let her complete the training programme.

All of the money the women can earn is absorbed by their families' immediate needs; none is saved. There is great resistance to the suggestion made by Swagata and Mandira that they open bank accounts and try to save a percentage of their earnings. The women's main reason for working is their desire to improve their families' standard of living and they cannot see the advantages of saving, even though the money might enable them to cover a family emergency without recourse to the ever-present money-lenders. They are only concerned with present needs. A regular programme of saving is necessary if the women are to become economically independent and develop a sense of control over their own lives, but a desire for such control does not develop quickly in women who have for centuries been conditioned to dependence and self-sacrifice.

The Kolaghat Socio-Economic Welfare Society has grown since 1984 and now includes not only the tailoring group but also women and men involved in other income-generation schemes such as poultry raising. The society has a programme of community health care and a legal cell. Dipali, the young unmarried leader of the women's group, is also a member of the legal cell. At the women's meeting (held in a small room the society rents as an office, workroom and venue for meetings and training) Dipali tells of a problem recently solved by the cell. A barren women asked her husband to take a second wife but then found herself becoming the target of beatings and abuse from both the new wife and her husband. Finally she ran away, but after women from the legal cell visited the husband and discussed the situation, the first wife was able to return and the beatings stopped.

Squeezing the soft sweets into pieces with her right

hand and distributing them among the women crowded on the mat, is Smita. A few days after her marriage she discovered that her husband was a drunkard who frequently beat her when he returned home late at night. After one and a half years of marriage, Smita discovered that her husband was maintaining another woman in a separate house. When the woman paid a visit to Smita's sister-in-law one day, carrying her baby daughter in her arms, she was cordially received while Smita stood in the background consumed with anger and jealousy. When she confronted her husband that night, she was severely beaten and the next day returned home to her parents. With SLARTC's help she eventually obtained a divorce, but she is still wearing the Bengali symbols of marriage – red and white bangles, a *sindur* dot on her forehead and a streak of red in the parting of her hair – so the villagers won't insult her. Her parents have also threatened to marry her off again if she discards these outward signs of respectability.

When the group is asked how many of their members are married, they count the women wearing bangles and *sindur*, and include Smita in the tally, even though they know she is divorced. Swagata turns to Smita, urging her to throw her bangles away, to wash her forehead. Her refusal to accept her husband's cruelty was brave but she must not stop half way to independence. Some of the members chorus their support of this idea, others sit and stare at the mat. They won't say what they would do in Smita's place. Swagata promises her the support of the other women and of SLARTC if her parents try to force her into remarriage. Smita twists the bangles of contention around and around her wrists but she will not remove them today.

It will take time before Smita discards her bangles but Rekha, another member of the group, has started a literacy course for women in her village and their enthusiasm is so great that they often study late into the night. It will take time before the women brave family censure and their own feelings of guilt to begin putting a few rupees in the bank each month, but already they are planning to save time and money by harvesting each other's land co-operatively. It will take even more time before society ceases to condone the ill treatment of women and before the poor are enabled to seek and obtain justice, but through the work of SLARTC more and more people are becoming aware of the legal rights they already have and of their power as a group not only to demand legal justice, but to secure other basic human rights such as education, economic independence and self-respect.

As we return, driving towards the city, the full moon is rising in the evening sky. It is cool, almost the end of winter, and the land is waking up. Boys working in pairs lift water from the irrigation ditches to the fields, rhythmically swinging wide vessels on the end of ropes, while men operate more sophisticated structures with their feet. Herds of cows amble into the traffic, and women walk in pairs or small groups towards home. Some are wearing the yellow sarees of spring.

The Need for Legal Education and Legal Aid

by Manabendra Mandal

Article 39A of the Constitution of India provides for equal, just and free legal aid. Since this article was added to the Constitution, most of the state governments have made enactments and set up Legal-Aid Boards and Committees. The provision of the Constitution ensures that opportunities for securing justice are not denied to any citizen who are financially or otherwise disadvantaged. In reality, ordinary people look more towards Voluntary

Legal Aid than the government-sponsored legal aid schemes. The people have offered their own reasons for this choice, principally that many of the cases are against the government itself and they fear that the government-panelled lawyers for legal aid cases may not dare to speak out against the government. Another problem is that the typical delays and other bureaucratic procedures make them feel frustrated. However, we do not want to comment on this as people are the best judge of any system.

In the creation of legal and social awareness amongst the common people, voluntary organizations such as ours have played a dominant role by organizing training courses, seminars, workshops, day-schools, etc. In India, voluntary organizations have played a vital part in ameliorating the distress of the poor and uneducated classes.

Without legal aid, legal justice will remain only a daydream for the poor and down-trodden. They simply do not have the means to attain legal justice. Legal aid organizations, both government and non-government, should make an all-out effort to ensure that justice is brought to the doorstep of the poor and down-trodden, and that bureaucratic barriers and lengthy formal procedures are no longer allowed to act as a barrier to the provision of justice for these people.

Today, social and legal justice is not readily available to ordinary people. Fifty per cent of the people in India live either below or marginally above the poverty line. The expenses involved and the time consumed in legal cases prevent them from getting justice through a court of law. For example, if a villager working as a day labourer has to attend a court of law (which is invariably in the town) he will lose his daily earnings. He will have to bear the costs of transport and meals for both himself and his witnesses. Moreover, he will have to pay the lawyer's fees and other court expenses. Not having any savings to bank upon, he often takes a loan from the local *mahajan* (money-lender) usually at an exorbitant rate of interest. As a result, instead of getting his grievances redressed, he gets into debt.

In a country like ours where the average literacy rate is below 40 per cent, the teaching of legal awareness and legal literacy is vital if people want to live with respect and dignity in society. If people know their legal rights and duties, there is a chance that they will be exploited less. Legal awareness programmes will help create faith and self-confidence about legal rights and this will encourage the people to fight against the exploitation and injustice that they experience.

5. Community Rehabilitation of the Disabled in India by Viklang Kendra

by Dr B. Banerji (founder of Viklang Kendra), Dr Malcolm Peat, and others.

Viklang Kendra is an Indian organization specializing in the rehabilitation of the rural disabled in India. It is based in Allahabad and has pioneered work in this field and especially with appropriate levels of rehabilitative technology that are within the reach of its patients. This chapter consists of two parts: a report on a trip made by Dr Malcolm Peat of Queens University School of Rehabilitative Medicine in Kingston, Canada (Queens University has an ongoing programme of assistance to Viklang Kendra); and extracts from Viklang Kendra's tenth anniversary commemorative magazine.

Current Services for the Physically Handicapped in South and South-East Asia (and a visit to Viklang Kendra)

by Dr Malcolm Peat

It is well established that the disabled population of these regions lack adequate rehabilitation services. In general, facilities are concentrated in urban areas with little or no activity at the rural or community level. Specialized urban services, such as those available in institutions in Bombay, Bangkok and Rangoon, offer a wide variety of clinical facilities of satisfactory to excellent standards. However,

The Five Characteristics of Poor People

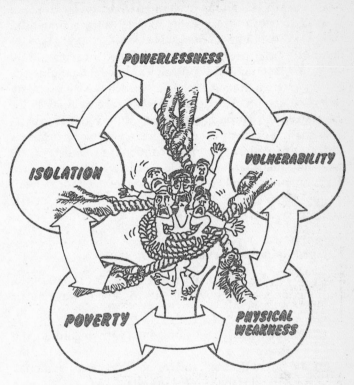

Source: Robert Chambers, *Rural Development – Putting the Last First* (Longman: London, 1983); adapted by the Local Government Training II programme in Indonesia and used in Richard Holloway and David Watson (eds), *Changing Focus – Involving the Rural Poor in Development Planning* (Oxford and IBH Publishing: New Delhi, 1989).

these locations cannot satisfy the widespread nature of demand for such services.

A major difficulty in the development of programmes for the physically handicapped has been that clinical services have been based upon a European/North American model of institutional care. The disadvantages of this are now clearly identified, as the system emphasizes institutional roles and does little or nothing to involve the community, family and the disabled themselves in the clinical management and social integration of the disabled into community life. The "institutional" approach to rehabilitation service development, although easy to criticize now, was for many years the accepted model for the delivery of services for the physically handicapped. South and South-East Asia now share a concern expressed widely in North America and Europe of how to "de-institutionalize" much of the care and management of the disabled and emphasize the community/family component so that the improvement in quality of life for the handicapped can occur at the community level.

The provision of services

Overcoming the inadequacies of services for the disabled can be addressed by governments in several ways including:

(i) national policy developments with regard to the disabled;

(ii) the identification and establishment of national/provincial/state/country priorities; *and*

(iii) the development of new categories of health care personnel.

However, it has become apparent that significant developments and improvements must involve the broad spectrum of non-government and community resources. The current situation is compounded by the fact that governments lack the resources in finance and personnel to effect any major changes or improvements in services/programmes for the physically handicapped – particularly in the area of community programmes. Any government-sponsored improvements in the delivery of health care will continue to be in the areas of institutional medicine and in broad national programmes for areas such as nutrition, clean water, and the immunization of children. Although WHO (the World Health Organization) has been advocating the development of community-based programmes for the physically handicapped, there is currently no clear evidence that this is becoming the accepted focus for rehabilitation service development.

Other than the general lack of government resources, the established rehabilitation professionals have been less than enthusiastic about the development of community-based programmes. The training of aides, and/or community rehabilitation "workers", is seen as a threat to "established" practice. The health-care professionals, although agreeing to the concept of community-based programmes, insist that services must be provided by fully trained personnel and not by aides or other categories of partly trained individuals. This is an argument which is by no means new in the delivery of health care in developing societies. Similar arguments have been raised about the provision of medical and nursing personnel. The literature of health-service development is full of examples of the conflict between professional protection of status and the actual needs of the broader community. The Third World is not the only area of this conflict.

Viklang Kendra

This is a unique institution, evolved over a period of approximately 15 years, offering a wide range of in-patient, out-patient and community services. It is organized and run by a group of highly motivated individuals under the leadership of Dr J. B. Banerji. Through the persistence of a small core of health professionals the centre can now provide a comprehensive rehabilitation service including:

a Surgical/orthopaedic service
Physiotherapy

Occupational therapy
Prosthetics and orthotics
Special education

In addition to the above institutionally based services, Dr Banerji and his colleagues are developing an "out-reach" community-based programme. Another unique feature of the institution is the attempt to use local materials in the design and production of orthotic and prosthetic devices.

The Viklang Kendra is an outstanding example of a non-government endeavour to develop and provide a level of service for the physically handicapped, with an emphasis on the development of a comprehensive approach with strong effective community participation.

The strengths of this approach are quite clear, and the description above attempts to identify the essential aspects of the programme. The difficulties encountered by Dr Banerji and his colleagues are related to the clinical approaches and techniques being used by various personnel. In some instances they are using clinical techniques which have elsewhere undergone considerable modification and development in recent years. Discussions clearly indicate that the centre and its constituent services would derive considerable benefits from an academic and clinical link with personnel in similar areas of practice, and with similar views of development. Dr Banerji and his colleagues have limited access to advances in clinical practice which would enhance the development of the activities at both the institutional and community level. As this is an NGO concern, access to local and national government resources is severely limited.

Disability and Rehabilitation

by Dinesh Mohan

When designing rehabilitation services in developing

countries, the following issues should be kept in mind:

(i) Rehabilitation services need to be decentralized. Institutional care is very expensive and if the time spent in institutions is reduced, the total cost per patient comes down and more people can be served; centralized rehabilitation services are not easily accessible and, furthermore, in some societies cultural factors make it easier for certain functions in rehabilitation to be performed at home. Training programmes for such systems should be developed.

(ii) Expensive aids reach few people. Aids should be made as simple, reliable and inexpensive as possible. By reducing complexity, there is less likelihood of failure, and maintenance is also easier. Poor people do not find it easy to return to clinics to have their aids repaired, so they just stop using them.

(iii) Disability need not be hidden. There has long been an assumption that one of the most important functions of rehabilitation or the design of an aid is to hide the disability. Some recent studies suggest that this need not be true for all kinds of disability or for all individuals. In some cases, not hiding the disability may make the aid cheaper. More importantly, it may be easier for the persons whose disability is visible to function in society, as other people can make adequate adjustments.

(iv) The needs of the disabled themselves are the main concern and aids should be designed according to their expressed needs and wishes. Very often, engineers and medical professionals design aids according to what they themselves consider important. They may even introduce more complexity into the design, not because the disabled consider it necessary, but because complexity is more exciting for the professionals.

(v) Aids should be designed so that their manufacture

and fitting times are minimized. Poor people do not have much time to waste in clinics, and a large proportion of the disabled in developing countries are poor. Their employers (if any) or the employers of their relatives, do not allow much time off and looking after a relative at the clinic may pose a heavy economic burden.

(vi) The disabled should be integrated into mainstream society. Professionals dealing with rehabilitation services are slowly realizing that services like sheltered workshops are not very effective or economical. They also reach very few people.

While these considerations are known to be important, it has not been easy to incorporate them into rehabilitation services. There are notable exceptions in some countries where excellent work is being done, but by and large the rehabilitation of the disabled has been neglected by policy-planners and scientists alike.

Unless inexpensive aids are developed which can be made by local artisans, a vast proportion of the disabled population in developing countries will remain unserviced. Short pamphlets should be published which would help people to make many aids locally. Given below are some of the aids which need to be designed and manufactured on a large scale in developing countries:

(i) For the hearing and speech disabled: solar-powered hearing aids with very few controls; job-specific hearing aids for vocational rehabilitation; voice-pattern instructors; vibrotactile aids, etc. Acoustic characterization of languages other than English needs to be done so that hearing aids can be designed for specific cultural needs.

(ii) For the visually disabled: low-cost Braille writers in different languages; Braille duplicators; talking books; Braille maps; lightweight folding canes with lighted or luminescent points; low-vision aids; recreational aids; teaching aids; microchip technology adapted to produce auditory information about items of daily use, such as watches, calculators, and thermometers, etc.

(iii) For the locomotor disabled: rapid fit prostheses; squatting and floor-sitting prostheses; light and less cumbersome orthoses; calipers which are lighter and more suited to tropical climates; portable mobility devices for uneven surfaces.

Our First Rural Rehabilitation Unit – at Bairampur Village

by Shri A.P. Singh

The Rural Unit based at Bairampur Village of Manjhanpur Tehsil of Allahabad District covers 22 villages in a radius of four kilometres, with a combined population of 21,000 including 247 orthopaedically handicapped people.

It is commonly believed that the rehabilitation of the physically handicapped is the prerogative of city-based, sophisticated centres. We wanted to remove this mystique. The main aims were to make the villagers come forward to look after the handicapped of their own village and to mobilize to the fullest possible extent, the locally available raw materials and skills; and to give a guiding hand at critical junctures – so that a package of services is created by the village itself for the rehabilitation of its own handicapped people. Furthermore, we wanted to create an environment where the villagers themselves would want to prevent the occurrence of diseases and subsequent impairment and disabilities. This is our concept of rehabilitation.

Our Base Unit, called Viklang Kendra, was built exactly according to this philosophy. Centred in a tin-shed, it exists on low-budget technology, which was generated exclusively from within the community. Its innovativeness, and the resources that it can mobilize (skilled labour and materials) were based, and are still being based, totally on the community. The mainstay of our financial support is still the two or three rupees given by *rickshawallahs* and *panwallahs* (rickshaw operators and people selling "pan", a betel nut concoction used as a digestive). The help from local service clubs is also valuable. The fact that these resources come from within the community for people who are handicapped, but who belong in their very own community, and that the community itself feels responsible for stopping future disabilities, has given the Viklang Kendra a tremendous resilience to work against all conceivable odds. Its innovativeness and ability to work under varying conditions are reproducible at all levels – particularly the rural level.

Having seen and closely studied the health situation in India and in most Third World countries, we felt that creation of a cadre of super professionals is not the answer to our rural-based health problems. It was found imperative to involve people belonging to their own villages, and give them a training package which they could easily implement at their own homes in the villages. They would need specialized guidance at critical junctures only. Also, a system of communication and referral, and a central unit for co-ordination had to be formed which could organize the entire village-level work. This was the fundamental objective of the project. *The aim is not only rehabilitation of the physically handicapped in the area but also to exert disability control so that no more disabilities occur.*

This venture is novel because until now in India, there have been no rural rehabilitation programmes based in rural areas for the physically handicapped and for disability control. So this is the first of its kind in India.

What makes this programme interesting is the help that has been offered including the Unit, a big building that was given by Shri Bhanu Pratap Singh (not the Minister) in Village Bairampur; and the voluntary involvement of school teachers, *gaon pradhans* (village leaders), village social workers, practitioners of all kinds of medicine, the village *purkhins* (matrons whose opinions are respected), the village-level workers, Auxiliary Nurse-Midwives (ANMs), and all the block-level workers (including the Primary Health Centre who are involving themselves of their own accord). An idea that we thought would be scoffed at became a kind of a mass movement. It is true that organizing all these workers, primarily through our band of three village-level rehabilitation workers (trained at the Base Unit), and co-ordinating the work with the Base Unit, requires a tremendous amount of organization – particularly taking into account the variables which exist in all rural work.

Unfortunate facts like a disabled child who would be given no place to sleep in the house of a villager, while the cow will be provided with a special shed, are interesting, tragic and brutally realistic features of the micro-level socio-economic situation of the handicapped in rural areas. To sell new ideas to such people and to overcome village politics is not an easy task, but it is a very challenging one. "Service" is a concept which cuts across barriers of many kinds and the devotion and missionary spirit provided at the Base Unit are the redeeming feature. Indeed, the use of missionary service (by "missionary" I mean a devotional not a religious approach) and motivation factors in organization, planning and administration at the rural level could make an interesting case study in social and economic phenomena at the village level. One always has to ask why it is that a centre which is hardly worth the name – from the point of view of its building and equipment – has so many patients while a Primary Health Centre with all its amenities remains a fossilized reminder of inappropriate medical technology.

As is true with all such programmes, much enthusiasm

exists in the initial phases but gradually the barometric depression comes: we are not being overtly idealistic about the situation as we wait for more long-term results to emerge. But we are sure that we shall make it work and, mind you, not just on paper. Far more inputs are necessary in the form of recurring finance and equipment, both in the Base Unit and the Rural Unit, in order to achieve a greater degree of operational efficiency. But what has been realized under existing limitations, we can say with all humility, is no small achievement.

Above all, this project serves as a model for the entire Third World, both for replication and study, because it is geared to the simple primary rehabilitation needs of the physically handicapped and minimizes the need for highly trained workforces and sophisticated equipment, so avoiding becoming an expensive, unused monument to medical technology.

Indigenously Devised Splints and Adaptations Designed to suit the Local Environment and Needs

by Dr W.G. Rama Rao

Anxious to adopt what is tried and approved by the accident experts, it is not surprising that the All India Institute of Physical Medicine and Rehabilitation (AIIPMR), situated in a metropolitan city like Bombay, automatically adopted western technology and therapy in rehabilitating the physically handicapped.

India is rich, in its tradition, its culture and its beliefs, but the people are poor. The simplicity of Indian life, its traditional clothing, ways of bathing and use of the toilet, food and utensils, its geography and its economic problems, are not given sufficient consideration. Forgotten is the fact that, in our country, the family is a very stable social institution; the majority of the people live in the rural areas and are dependent on an agricultural economy which provides for a large number of semi-skilled and unskilled occupations; and the culture as a whole encourages collective, co-operative endeavours with very little emphasis on the competitive strivings of the individual. All this facilitates the integration of the handicapped into the community and a large number of the handicapped are not perceived as "problems" by those around them.

Unlike the city-dwellers, the 400-odd million rural population is slow to accept sophisticated ideas for equipment. This is not because they are dull-witted but because drastic change, however rational and effective, is not acceptable to the rural community and so to the patient. It is not because people cannot be motivated through reason; language is not necessarily the way to communicate with these tradition-bound people, there is something more. If a programme has to be successful, it must accept a special sort of communication in order to involve them.

Within the programme of the AIIPMR we have a decade of effective training, teaching and therapeutic programmes behind us; we have 560 physiotherapists and occupational therapists, 200 rehabilitation nurses, 150 medical personnel, and 60 prosthetic and orthotic technicians from the Institute carrying on rehabilitation work. However, recently we asked ourselves a pertinent question:

"Does the assistance that we offer serve the Rehabilitation Programme horizontally as well as vertically? Do we assist the optimum functioning of the handicapped in their own environment, spreading this care on a large scale, socially as well as geographically?"

Our statistical survey revealed discouraging results. Almost 50 per cent of the technical aid and advice was not used. It was important to know why this was so.

Owing to geographical and economic factors, there often is little communication between various workers in the country. We wanted to discover if this was the experience of others or if, unnoticed by us, people are engaged in an original way of doing useful things for the handicapped, and if there were possibilities which required only a relatively small financial or technical improvement. Thus we recently organized a representative workshop at the Institute. The following were our findings:

(i) We realized that the handicapped should be helped to function within their own environment and all efforts should be directed towards that goal with a minimum of means and maximum of inventiveness.

(ii) Technical aids cannot and should not be ends in themselves. They should be effective in our rural environment and make things easier for handicapped persons to manage the situations they meet in everyday life in the home and at work, indoors as well as outdoors.

(iii) A major drawback in the adoption of the borrowed technical aids has been no thorough analysis of what one should be able to demand of the aid in a rural situation in our country. Even simple gadgets that are commonly used in the western world can't fulfil the requirements of the average patient in our country. The need for research in this area is great.

(iv) The aid must be kept as simple as possible, even if it involves sacrificing 100 per cent mechanical efficiency, to achieve continuing use or the possibility of replacement.

(v) Things that are traditionally accepted, particularly on religious grounds, must be evaluated and subtle changes may be incorporated to make the aid more adequate or effective.

(vi) One should explore aids devised by the patient out of necessity, measure and compare these various innovations, and improve on them while keeping the cost within the easy reach of rural patients.

Current technological development makes possible things which, 10 or 20 years ago, seemed totally impossible but, to my mind, there doesn't seem to be a place for "developing" countries as far as technology is concerned. "Indigenous technological know-how" must be explored for improving aids, albeit for the future. A large investment in the development of aids is a worthwhile venture for any country; it will have a noticeable effect on the economy of the country by creating an opportunity for employment and the possibility of an export market.

The Indian government spent more than 40 million rupees on creating an industrial complex, ALIMCO at Kanpur, to meet the needs of the country's handicapped. But ALIMCO should also continue to explore the functionally workable and economically viable contraptions prepared by voluntary organizations all over the country, using abundantly available indigenous materials. Where possible, these models should also be made cheaper and more efficient. It is essential to realize that what is being used by the handicapped person is worth copying, marginally improving mechanical efficiency where that can be done.

6. Overthrowing the Money-Lenders

by S.P. Wikramaratchi

S.P. Wickramaratchi is an action researcher with the PIDA (Participatory Institute for Development Alternatives) in Sri Lanka. This NGO recently won the Right Livelihood Award for its work with the rural and urban poor. This chapter was originally published in *Development*, the journal of the Society for International Development, no. 2, 1984.

A "neutral" or technocratic intervention by government or non-government organizations in village development often results in only the dominant interest in the village benefiting. On the other hand, participators who act as catalysts in intervention programmes succeed in their objective, as the people described in this article did when they escaped from the clutches of the money-lenders.

Village society in Sri Lanka is not a homogeneous or a harmonious entity, it is one that is full of basic contradictions. On the one hand there is a minority representing the dominant interest – the traders, money-lenders, the bigger landowners, the élite in general and even the village-level bureaucrats – who benefit from the status quo. On the other is the majority, consisting of the small and marginal farmers, landless workers, small fisher folk, rural artisans and others who live in poverty.

Relations between two groups are often asymmetrical in form and take on an unequal, dominant–dependent character with the rich able to control the very survival of the poor. As a result, a considerable portion of the

The Government's View of the Poor and the Poor's View of Themselves, Concerning Money

THE POOR DO NOT KNOW HOW TO LOOK AFTER THEIR MONEY AND SAVE IT

FAMILY SICK

TAKE VERY ARDUOUS WAGE-LABOUR AT LOW PAY

SELL GOODS QUICKLY AT A CHEAP PRICE

BORROW MONEY AT CRIPPLING INTEREST RATE

SHORT OF CASH – BORROW MONEY AT HIGH INTEREST

FAMILY FACES CALAMITY, SALE OF CROP USED TO PAY OFF INTEREST, GREAT NEED FOR MORE MONEY

UNABLE TO REPAY LOAN, SELL CROP IN THE FIELD BEFORE HARVEST AT A LOW PRICE

Source: Richard Holloway and David Watson (eds), *Changing Focus – Involving the Rural Poor in Development Planning* (Oxford and IBH Publishing: New Delhi, 1989).

production value of the small producer (whether farmer, fisherfolk, artisan or wage earner) ultimately ends up in the hands of the dominant interests. This occurs through low prices being paid for produce, high prices charged for inputs, high land rents, low wages, exorbitant interest rates, and various sorts of corruption.

The drain of the economic surplus in production through the dependency links, leads to the further impoverishment of the poor, suppresses the rural production forces, and keeps the production of the poor at a low level. In this context it is natural that dependency attitudes are intensified among the rural poor as well as in the social structure of the village. Moreover, the poor themselves are not a homogeneous category. They are divided by caste, religion and other issues, and compete with each other for the limited economic opportunities in the village. Dependency attitudes and lack of unity inhibit them from taking initiatives to improve their lot and tend to make them non-innovative and non-experimental.

Under these circumstances a delivered, "neutral" or technocratic intervention, whether by government or even a non-governmental organization, working on the harmony model can only end up by adjusting to the dynamics of the contradictions in the village society and thus often benefiting the dominant interests, with only a marginal trickle down, if any at all. This explains why it is difficult, if not impossible, for self-reliant rural development to be a spontaneously generated process and why catalytic intervention is more often than not a necessary initial input to stimulate the poor to take self-reliant action. A committed catalyst, who is able to identify with the poor, can enter village communities and carry out preliminary investigations of village society through a process of direct observations and informal interactions with the people.

First, they identify the poorer sections of the village society, and stimulate them to get together to investigate and analyse their own reality, and the reality of the village situation. In particular, people are stimulated to identify and examine the factors that continue to keep them in poverty and to ask if there are any elements operating within their environment which they could change. In the case of small-producer peasants, for example, such investigation and analysis have often focused on the income losses they suffer as a result of their dependency relations with traders, money-lenders, land-owners, and other dominant interests in the village society. Quite often these poor persons can quantify the extent of their income losses by using simple arithmetic. In this way, the interaction between the catalytic intervener and the community sparks off a certain chemistry – people initiate a process of scientific inquiry into their poverty. They move away from a sensory perception of their poverty to a conceptual and analytical framework, for their deliberations begin to relate their poverty to the social environment around them.

Such a build up of awareness is often followed by a search for actions that the poor themselves can undertake together, using their own skills and meagre resources, to counter the process of impoverishment that they have identified. They systematically ask themselves whether the social and economic reality of the village situation which has reproduced poverty can be changed in their favour and if so, how. The small-producer peasants, for example, would begin to explore what means are available within their collective power to retain the surplus of their production, to protect it from exploiters, and to use it for their own consumption and investment. For this, they need to form a group and initiate action to eliminate their dependency relations, which are the source of the surplus drain. It becomes clear that if they acted individually they would be too weak to start such self-reliant action.

Organized people's groups emerge as a logical outcome of this process. A collective fund to which each member contributes a small sum of money (however small it may be at the beginning) is often the first action that such groups undertake. People begin to experiment with alternative ways of increasing the share of the production they could retain and with ways of increasing the total production value itself. Every action is followed by collective reflection and analysis so that the subsequent action is improved. With each action, the group fund expands and people begin to improve their access to resources and the people's confidence in their ability to change the reality is also enhanced. Thus, a process of self-reliant development is initiated.

The Ranna story

The village in Ranna is situated about 130 miles away from Colombo city in the southern province of Sri Lanka. Of the total population, more than 90 per cent are subsistence farmers who could be categorized into two groups:

(i) Peasant farmers who cultivate highlands without irrigation facilities, depending entirely upon the rains; *and*

(ii) Peasant farmers who cultivate paddy in the settlement areas with irrigation facilities.

These farmers are mainly occupied with the cultivation of vegetables and other food crops on their one to one-and-a-half acre plots, in the two seasons. The main vegetables cultivated include snake gourds, luffa gourds, ladies' fingers (okra), brinjals (aubergines), tomatoes, beans and curry chillies; the food crops are cowpea, green grams, groundnuts, maize, etc. The produce is taken by the cultivator himself to the nearest town fair (market) for sale. These market centres have thus become the contact point between the farmer and the buyer. In addition, there are sales points in these centres for all kinds of agricultural inputs such as fertilizers and agrochemicals.

The money-lenders and brokers, who link up the farmer

with the buyers who come from cities, also operate in these centres where the system of exploitation of the small farmer-producer is deeply rooted. The money-lender provides loans at exorbitant interest rates for the farmer's produce, as well as for their living expenses. This process is perpetuated as the small farmer-producer can never repay the debt and becomes totally dependent upon the money-lender.

As an example, let us see how a small farmer-producer gets into the grip of the money-lender. An analysis of a typical expenditure pattern of a small farmer reveals the following:

AGRICULTURAL INPUT	Rs. cts.
1. Sticks for fencing, etc., including transport	300.00
2. Coir yarn (800 bundles: approximately 150 kg)	1,200.00
3. Wire (50 kg)	900.00
4. Pesticides (5 bottles at 118 rupees each)	590.00
TOTAL	2,990.00

Since the small farmer-producer is without this basic capital he has to put himself at the mercy of the money-lender in order to obtain loans at an interest rate of 20 per cent per month. As a result, for the capital he has taken, the small farmer has to pay back in interest about 1,800 rupees for the period of three months until he harvests his crops. On the other hand, the small farmer-producer is not blessed with proper irrigation facilities and depends on the rain. He therefore has to use additional farm labourers to start his cultivation as soon as the rains start. For this he has to borrow 1,000 rupees with an interest rate of 20 per cent a month, for three months. This means that the farmer spends 1,600 rupees.

It is very clear that, as a result of this system, the average farmer cultivating one acre of highland has to spend 2,990 rupees of capital on cultivation plus 1,000 rupees on hired labour and 2,760 rupees on domestic consumption. This gives a total cost of 6,750 rupees – a sum which carries an interest charge of 4,056 rupees. The small farmer has to face several other threats as well. When he goes to the market to sell his produce, he has to pay the commission agent eight per cent, and the market fees collector three per cent. The buyers purposely use low weights in their scales thereby cheating the farmer of another two per cent. The amount required to pay the hired labour is also borrowed from the money-lenders and the farmer has to pay an interest of 600 rupees per month on this, too. The brokers also keep a cut of about four to five per cent from the actual prices; that is paid by the wholesale buyers. As a result, a small farmer has to (knowingly or unknowingly)

LABOUR COSTS	Rs. cts.
1. Jungle clearing, weeding, etc., for five people at 25 rupees per person for three days	375.00
2. Preparation of the beds for five people per day at 25 rupees per person per day	125.00
3. Tilling the soil – five people per day at 25 rupees per day for two days	250.00
4. Weeding after one month for five people at 25 rupees per day for two days	250.00
TOTAL	1,000.00

HOUSEHOLD EXPENSES/CONSUMPTION
EXPENDITURE PER WEEK FROM THE TIME OF
CULTIVATION TO THE HARVESTING PERIOD
(These figures were taken from a household that
consists of five members)

	Rs. cts.
1. 17.5 kg rice	05.00
2. 14 coconuts	70.00
3. 1 kg sugar	12.50
4. 150 g tea leaves	12.50
5. 2 litres kerosene oil	14.50
6. 100 g spices for curries	4.50
7. 500 g peppers	3.00
8. 500 g red onions	85.00
TOTAL FOR ONE WEEK	230.00

spend about another 17 per cent of his produce through
the exploitative sales system. This results in a further loss
of 2,500 rupees.

Even though a farmer who cultivates one acre of land
could get a return of about 15,000 rupees per season, he has
to spend about 13,366 rupees on all his debts, consumption
and leakages. The balance left for his entire family, for
children's education, housing, health facilities, and other
social obligations is only 1,634 rupees for another three
months.

Under irrigation

The situation of the paddy farmer who cultivates with
irrigation facilities is even worse (see the table below).

PADDY CULTIVATION – REQUIRED CAPITAL FOR ONE ACRE OF PADDY FOR ONE SEASON	
	Rs. cts.
1. Ploughing by tractor at 45 rupees for three ploughs	450.00
2. Hired labour for preparing paddy fields in addition to own labour	250.00
3. Fertilizer: 3.5 cwt of Urea TDM and Ammonium Sulphate	525.00
4. Weedicide/Pesticide spraying. Spray machine charges (five times per season at 20 rupees per spray)	100.00
5. Weedicides	315.00
6. Pesticides	250.00
7. Seed Paddy at 95 rupees per bushel for three bushels	285.00
TOTAL	2,175.00

Since this capital input is not available from the farmers' own resources, they also take loans from the village money-lender. When loans are taken for paddy cultivation, farmers have to pay back the loans in paddy. For the capital input loan a farmer has to pay 52 bushels of paddy which is equivalent to 1,144 kg. In this case the interest is also calculated in a very exploitative manner. For every 250 rupees a farmer takes as a loan, he has to give two bushels (22 kg × 2) of paddy which costs about 450 rupees in the open market.

During the period of cultivation, the paddy farmer has to take another loan for his family consumption. This generally comes to about 1,000 rupees for which the interest is again about 24 bushels, that is equivalent to 528 kg of paddy. An average farmer who cultivates one acre of paddy spends about 3,175 rupees for capital inputs and for household consumption. The loan repayment in paddy is 76 bushels which is equivalent to 1,672 kg.

As a result of this unfortunate situation, the farmer faces three major problems. As soon as he harvests his crop he has to return the loans taken from the money-lender in paddy. This means that he loses the chance of selling his paddy in the open market at a competitive price. He is now compelled to take loans from the village money-lenders and falls into a bonded situation where his crop or his labour is permanently mortgaged to the money-lender. Elaborating on the simple arithmetic of this we find that:

(i) During the harvesting season six bushels of paddy (132 kg) are worth about 450 rupees on the open market. But the agreement between the money-lender and the farmer prevents him from selling it outside; thus he loses 200 rupees for every six bushels (132 kg) when repaying his loan. The total amount he loses is 2,500 rupees.

(ii) After one month of the harvesting season, the paddy prices in the open market rise to about 600–650 rupees per 6 bushels (132 kg). This way, since the farmer has paid his debts in paddy, he cannot keep any to be sold when the prices are high. Therefore he loses another 1,875 rupees. In all the paddy farmer loses a total amount of 4,375 rupees for taking 2,175 rupees as a loan from the money-lenders during the cultivation period.

(iii) The other unforeseen and unfortunate factors are the climatic disasters that occur. If the farmer's crop is damaged or his yield goes below the average anticipated, he is compelled to mortgage his land to

the money-lenders, and become a wage earner on
his own land under the money-lender.

(iv) In the presence of this vicious circle of exploitation and dependency, the highland farmer who
cultivates vegetables, or the paddy farmer who
cultivates paddy with irrigation facilities, continue
in conditions of extreme poverty and semi-bondage
throughout their lives.

The impact of Participatory Action Research

As a result of sensitive interventions by committed action
researchers from the Participatory Institute of Development Alternatives (PIDA), the farmers who were in the
grip of outside vested interests and dominant élites in the
village, are now systematically analysing their situation.
As a PIDA action researcher, my experience in working
with small farmers has proved that small groups of about
10–15 aware and organized farmers are capable, through
self-reliance, of breaking the vicious cycle of poverty and
dehumanization. The process requires that small-farmer
groups collectively investigate, analyse and understand
the socio-economic reality of their lives. In other words,
they must increase their awareness of the reality of their
poverty. With such conscientization, small-farmer groups
begin to explore what measures they themselves should
undertake to improve their lives. These are measures
which are feasible and within their own ability to implement, and not those set by outsiders.

In the village of Ranna, 25 vegetable cultivators (small
producers) formed such a group and, as indicated, deeply
analysed their poverty situation. As a result, they realized
that unless they reduced the expenditure in cultivation,
they could not break the cycle. Accordingly, they started
sharing labour rather than hiring it from outside and
eliminated hired labour cost completely. In this way they

were able collectively to save 2,500 rupees per season. This experience was so encouraging that the farmers started a small collective farm which they cultivated in their leisure time as a group.

The income generated from this farm helped them to build up a common fund which they decided to deposit in a bank. They also discussed with the bank the possibility of breaking away from the money-lenders, and made strong arguments as to why the banks should support the process and assist the poorest groups such as themselves. At the end of the discussion the bank, which had not been helping them before, had to agree that they could provide their services to this category of farmers. The result was that for the first time they were able to raise bank loans of 2,000 rupees per person for cultivation.

This was the crucial point at which the small farmers were able to break away from the money-lenders. In order to manage with their limited resources, they jointly explored all the possibilities for reducing their expenditure. As a result they bought all agricultural inputs in bulk at wholesale prices, reduced their household expenditure by purchasing the consumer items in bulk at wholesale rates, and by-passed the village blackmarketeers and traders who had hitherto exploited them. This created a tremendous impact in the area and helped in the expansion of the process and the formation of six other similar groups.

At this stage, the farmer group came to learn that the lease on the town market centre (where they sell their produce) would be auctioned for the years 1984–85. This opportunity enabled the original seven groups to create interest among other fellow farmers, and build up 19 farmer groups in 19 villages. There were 300 farmers in these groups and they met in one place to discuss their strategy to capture the market centre which was in the hands of a few capitalist traders, who were exploiting them. This also paved the way for them to strengthen their solidarity and form a federation which is known as the Ranna Region Vegetable Producers Association.

After several strategies and counter-strategies were tried, the Association employed the tactic of making an obviously very high bid and was able to capture the town market centre. In the previous year it was auctioned for 49,000 rupees; on this occasion the Association paid 80,000 rupees for it. There are several requirements to be fulfilled by the bidders when a market centre is auctioned. These are that:

   (i) they should deposit 10 per cent of the amount they have bid with the Development Council within 15 days from the day they have taken the tender;

  (ii) they should also pay the total amount in eight instalments; *and*

 (iii) they should pay two instalments plus 10 per cent of the total amount (28,000 rupees) within 15 days from the day they have taken the tender.

It was because of the inability to fulfil these basic requirements that the small farmer was unable earlier to capture the market centre. It is the same with all market centres in this area. As a result of group action, the savings they had made, and working in groups, the farmers managed the required saving to capture the market centre. At the end of the whole exercise they were able to make a profit of 30,000 rupees for themselves from the operations of the market centre and also to stay out of debt.

To co-ordinate the activities of the Association, two members from each group are nominated to serve for six months, allowing all members to participate. This committee meets once a month to discuss financial matters, other matters that concern the Association, problem areas and future programmes, etc. Just before the committee meeting, the village-level groups meet and discuss with their two representatives, the suggestions, proposals and problems to be considered at the committee meeting on behalf of their groups. This is also a two-way process. After the committee meeting, the village groups meet again to discuss the decisions of the committee. The ultimate result is that the village groups meet twice a month to discuss their problems and find new solutions on their own.

As a result of the capturing of the market centre, the brokers, middlemen and money-lenders were eliminated, and the farmers were able to deal directly with the wholesale buyers who came from outside. They also obtained better prices for their produce by building up their bargaining power. The farmers were able to stop the outflow of 17 per cent in paying commissions, undercuttings, market fees and losses incurred through underweighing. Instead, the Association now charges five per cent of the total value of sales as a service charge. This makes the Association self-financing and independent. From January to mid-June 1984, the amount collected was 160,760 rupees. This fund is now utilized to provide facilities for "soft loans" (those on easy terms) for production and also for consumer programmes for new village groups. There are now 26 village groups each with an Association and funds of their own savings from the village surplus.

The impact of this small-farmer action is now beginning to reach villages in the Districts. The farmers in new villages are becoming interested and are inviting the groups to help them organize and initiate the same process. It has also created a tremendous impact among the bureaucrats and bankers who are now willing to provide extension services, credit and all other governmental facilities to the small farmer through this Association, which grew up naturally and in response to the farmers' own needs.

The political leadership, which had earlier worked through the village élite, has begun to understand the process and are assuring this Association – a new style people's organization – of their co-operation and support.

7. Women of the Weeping Prairie – a Perspective on GRID, Thailand

by Janet Durno

GRID (Grass Roots Integrated Development) is a Thai consortium formed from three NGOs and a university department. It works in a very poor area of the North-East of Thailand called Thung Kula Ronghai ("The Weeping Prairie"). GRID practises an integrated form of development and tries to build up local people's organizations to decide upon, and then implement, the development of their choice. This article also includes a note on Participatory Integrated Rural Development in Thailand. Janet Durno, a consultant for CUSO and IDRC, was a onetime resident of Thailand whose language she speaks. This chapter was originally a paper written for CUSO.

Grandmother See was not born in Ban Som Hong but it is hard now for her to remember just how long she has lived here. Her family had moved three times already, looking for food, looking for land, and they found it finally in Som Hong. Perhaps 40 years ago, she says, leaning down to spit betel juice in a neat arc over the edge of the low wooden platform under the house on which everyone sits to talk in the cool shade. Her family was one of the first to arrive and, like the others, Lao-speaking migrants from Srisaket province. They claimed the land as they cleared it and now there are almost 50 houses in the village. It was all forest then, she remembers. There was water, there were animals, food was to be gathered everywhere. Today, she looks out across the road to where the dry field begins, knowing it stretches on and on. True, it is dotted with old and beautiful trees – shade-givers, fruit-bearers

The Government's View of the Poor and Poor's View of Themselves

Source: Richard Holloway and David Watson (eds), *Changing Focus – Involving the Rural Poor in Development Planning* (Oxford and IBH Publishing: New Delhi, 1989).

and fuel-providers – but the field rolls on and on and perhaps she would find that it never breaks against the feet of a forest again, not if she walked for the rest of her lifetime. For this is the Weeping Prairie – Thung Kula Ronghai.

Thung Kula Ronghai is a vast alluvial plain in the North-East of Thailand. Its people are farmers, the poorest in the country. They struggle to wrest a subsistence livelihood from sandy saline soils which may yield a scant half ton of rice per hectare; their crops are menaced by the droughts and flash-floods of an erratic monsoon. Many families cannot produce enough rice to last the year and at the beginning of the planting season must pledge the next harvest to borrow not only rice to eat but also expensive fertilizer to feed their fields. With interest rates as high as 100 to 150 per cent, these debts may never be paid off completely and continue to accumulate from year to year.

To a large extent, the villagers are victims of the world economy. Since 1981, the price of rice on the world market has been steadily declining and, with it, the already meagre incomes of Thai farmers. The US Farm Act, which allows the US government to purchase rice from American farmers at an inflated price and then sell it at a small fraction of the cost, will serve to lower prices even further. In addition, the Thai government's legislation setting a guaranteed minimum price for rice within the country is poorly enforced and thus consistently sidestepped by unscrupulous middlemen and large rice-mill owners.

With every year, the natural-resource base of the village diminishes. There are fewer fish and frogs and wild greens to be gathered. The land and the people grow poorer but the cost of living continues to rise. Government attempts to ameliorate the situation are often well-meant but are just as often unresponsive to the real needs of the poor or unsuccessful in actually reaching them. Programmes and services offered by government and NGOs are under-utilized as villagers are either unaware of the availability of assistance or, unsure how to secure it, lack the confidence to approach the confusing and awesome world of officialdom.

In the end, it is only the people themselves, intimately aware of their own physical and human environment, who can pinpoint their problems and work out viable solutions. Farmers who can no longer depend on the sale of rice, who find themselves growing poorer by the year must mobilize all their resources and draw on outside ones in order to diversify their agricultural practices, seek out alternative sources of income and build up the self-reliance of their community. One of the greatest of village resources still remains largely untapped: the bargaining and leverage potential of a united group. A catalyst is needed to set the process of participatory development in motion, to build up village leadership and community cohesion, to encourage village groups to tackle together the problems that they all have in common, and to facilitate linkages with sources of technical advice and financial assistance.

Such a catalyst has recently entered the Thung Kula Ronghai area in the form of the Grass Roots Integrated Development (GRID) Project, a programme mounted by four Thai agencies – The Appropriate Technology Association, The Graduate Volunteer Centre Alumni (GVCA), the Harry Durance Foundation, and the Research and Development Institute of Khon Kaen University. These agencies, which combine experience and expertise in the areas of appropriate technology, health, education, rural action research, evaluation and project implementation, began planning in 1982. They carried out a six-month field study of the region in 1983. In March 1984, Village Development Animateurs (VDAs) were placed in each of the six core villages to encourage the growth of community self-reliance and to assist the villagers in obtaining whatever support they require to implement their plans.

Kua is the VDA in Som Hong. Now in her mid-twenties, her interest in development work began at university where she spent more time working on Development Club projects than on her maths studies. After graduation, she spent a year as a Graduate Volunteer at a rural health station in the south of Thailand. It was at this time that Kua, the youngest child and only daughter of a middle-class Chiang Mai family, realized that she could cope with loneliness and the rigours of poverty, learning to conserve water, to eat unfamiliar food, to bathe in the canal with the villagers. In her next posting, as a United Nations Volunteer in Indonesia, she learned to speak Indonesian and to adapt to the foreign culture of the Islamic Javanese village in which she was placed. Finding the people of Java very different from Thais – often stubborn, selfish and narrow-minded – she was happy to return to Thailand after a year.

Through her association with GVCA, Kua was aware of the GRID project and acquainted with the staff. After returning from Indonesia she did some volunteer work with GRID promoting the use of herbal medicine and, when the first VDA placed in Som Hong left the project, she was asked to apply. Now she has been in Som Hong for one year, living first with the headman's family, then with another family, and now in her own little bamboo hut built against the side of the assistant headman's rice barn.

The work of a VDA appears very unstructured and amorphous to the villagers, especially at first. The VDA must get to know the people, collect data, develop an understanding of village problems and try to identify the informal leaders of the community and those with leadership potential. Many of the villagers are confused by the "foreigner" who has come to live among them; the villagers are of Laotian origin and retain many of their distinctive customs and traditions, so that a young educated urban-born Thai is almost as much of a novelty and mystery as a Canadian would be. Also unfamiliar is the emphasis on discussions, seminars and study tours to visit projects being carried out in other villages. In the past, most government development schemes have revolved around the construction of physical infrastructure such as dams, roads and wells; or they have been welfare-oriented, distributing blankets in the cold season or eucalyptus trees to plant for fuel. The villagers have naturally come to associate "development" with gifts and wonder why GRID does not also distribute such bounty. Slowly, however, some of the people are beginning to understand the concept of self-reliance, to realize that they themselves can take action to better their lives. Groups are being formed and the success of their small projects is encouraging further ventures.

It is the night before a wedding. Under and around the young groom's house, food for tomorrow's celebration is being prepared. Women wrap rice-flour sweets in banana leaves and roll tobacco in squares of old newspaper, tying the cylinders with filaments of yellow silk. Men chop pork in the big outdoor kitchen and meat sizzles in pans resting on little flower-pot charcoal-burning stoves. Young boys and girls are shredding bamboo shoots with thorn-tipped sticks. Music blares from the tape-recorder and some of the boys, tipsy from the rice whisky they have been drinking all evening, begin to dance. It is only a few steps before embarrassment overcomes them and they collapse, giggling, in a heap.

One of the men disappears into the darkness and suddenly returns holding a *khaen*, a traditional Laotian wind instrument made of graduated bamboo tubes, somewhat like the pipes of an organ. Another *khaen* appears, then a flute and a drum. As lightning flashes in the hot sky, the men sit cross-legged on the wooden platform and the vaguely Celtic strains of the Burma Axe Dance draw dancers from the shadows – not boys this time but rather two old and happy farmers, and a little madwoman in a short skirt. Some of the men clustered around the musicians dance sitting down, moving their arms and hands through the graceful gestures of the *ram wong* (a traditional Thai folk dance). Others clap along. Now it is "Lom Pat Prow" ("The Wind Blows the Coconut Leaves") and the madwoman sways lasciviously closer to her partners, both of whom spin absently away from her.

When the older men lose interest in the music, the teenaged members of the youth club band take over the instruments and soon a somewhat less polished version of "Lom Pat Prow" rises into the night. Kua helped the youth club to organize the band and find a teacher, and GRID purchased the instruments. After only three months' practice, the group has been hired to play at the ordination of a Buddhist monk in another village.

Almost all of the members of the Som Hong youth club are boys and there are no girls in the band. Although several girls signed up to study music, when the time came they were too shy to learn from a male teacher and to play music in public. A sewing class organized by Nee, a home-economics graduate from Chiang Mai, has been somewhat more successful. At present, blouses and shirts must be purchased in the town and village seamstresses could not only save their families money but also earn some extra income sewing for their neighbours. Nee began teaching the girls the basics of cutting and sewing clothes two months ago but, of the original 10 students, seven have already left to work in Bangkok, preferring to try their luck in the big city.

Members from an average of 30 per cent of these households migrate from Thung Kula Ronghai to work in Bangkok and other parts of the country for three to six months after the harvest is in. It is sheer poverty that drives the men to leave their families for the sugar-cane fields of Kanchanaburi or the construction sites of

Bangkok. Many of the young people, however, are as much drawn towards the adventure and excitement of the cities as impelled by the need of their families. But the weaving factories of Samut Prakan where most of Som Hong's youth find employment are no fairytale castles. From 7 a.m. to 9 p.m., six days a week, the girls operate looms and the boys work as mechanics. Room and board are provided along with a salary of 800 to 1,000 baht (US$ 30–35) a month. But even this minimal salary is good compared to that of other jobs; as a servant in a middle-class home for instance, a girl may work even longer hours and make only 400 baht a month. Most teenagers send almost their entire salary home to their parents. While many leave their jobs every year for several months to help with the planting and harvesting at home, others settle permanently in the city, returning only to visit.

Around mid-morning, the bus pulls into the grounds of the *wat* (the village temple) and a singing, drumming horde pours off. With powdered faces, paper flowers stuck behind their ears, and clad in stylish jeans and dresses, the young people disperse into the village to find their parents. Every year at this time the migrants return, some for a visit, some to stay, all bringing gifts and money to present to their parents and the *wat*. On this day also, the people celebrate the festival of Pra Wessandon, a prince exiled to the forest by his father for his excessive goodness to the poor, but eventually called back to take his place in his kingdom; in his next incarnation Pra Wessandon would become the Buddha.

The temple has become a bower, decorated with palm leaves and whole banana trees complete with roots. Small birds and fish, woven from leaves, sway in the breezes that blow through the open pavilion. Later in the afternoon – as loudspeakers in the temple grounds blast out "Girls Just Want to Have Fun" – the monks, saffron-orange robes brilliant against the dry colours of the field, lead the villagers in a chant beside a copse of trees. All return to the *wat* in a long procession, carrying bouquets of flowers and leaves, and walk round the temple placing the leaves in baskets hanging from the flagpoles. The streaming temple flags herald the return of Pra Wessandon who, like their children, has come to the village to bring happiness and luck for the coming year.

In the evening, another procession enters the *wat* bearing a money tree – a banana plant stuck in a pot of rice hung with notebooks, matches, packages of detergent and flowers made of ten baht notes (gifts for the monks). A wiry little man in jeans walks along playing the *khaen*, another man sings, an old lady dances as she walks and smiles, her betel-stained teeth like black seeds in her poppy-orange mouth.

Gifts to the *wat* bring merit to the givers. But nowadays, with the co-operation of the abbot, some of these gifts are being returned to the Som Hong community. Part of the money donated to the temple last year by villagers working in Bangkok was used by the village to dig a communal fish pond. Rice that would ordinarily be given to the *wat* is being used to fill a rice bank set up by the community, after a GRID study tour to another village convinced them of the bank's efficacy in combating debt. Rice from the rice bank is loaned to needy families at a lower rate of interest than they would have to pay if, as is usually the case, they borrowed rice from a money-lender in town. A Som Hong villager who borrows 10 *tung* (one *tung* = 20 litres) from the rice bank, must pay back 13 *tung* after the harvest whereas a money-lender would demand 15. The family is thus able to retain a larger portion of their harvest, while the interest swells the rice reserve and enables the bank to assist more families each year.

Projects such as the fish pond and the rice bank increase community self-reliance and confidence. The men who administer the projects develop leadership and management skills, and the ability to locate and contact outside sources of assistance. Plans are drawn up to address community problems. Groups are formed. But what of the women?

The strengthening of the village leadership is one of GRID's major objectives. However, when the Village Committee convenes a meeting the only woman present is Kua, whose education, experience and role as the VDA set her apart from the women of the village. Traditionally, women in the rural areas of Thailand have not taken a public role in the administration of village affairs. While this tradition is weakening in some other parts of the country and a few women have even been elected village headwomen, in the Lao villages of Thung Kula Ronghai the women remain content to play the role so vividly pictured in the old Thai saying: "Women are the hind legs of the elephant". The hind legs are just as important as the front legs in holding up the beast and they work just as hard, but they nevertheless walk behind. It has always been the men who have gone into the world and made contact with outsiders while the women have remained within the sphere of their individual families and homes.

So far, little progress has been made in encouraging the village women to form active groups or to involve themselves as village leaders, as the women do not perceive the necessity for such involvement. There is already a remarkable equality between men and women in the village society of Thung Kula Ronghai. Agricultural labour is shared, with women even taking part in such heavy work as ploughing and digging fish ponds. While housework still remains essentially a woman's job, men may also fetch water, wash clothes and occasionally help with the cooking. Family income is generally controlled by the wife and women make many of the family decisions. Women's opinions also strongly influence the course of community affairs as they take a vociferous part in the small informal discussions at which the decisions later ratified at formal meetings are really made. It never occurs to the majority of women to wonder if their interests are adequately represented or protected under the existing system.

Grandmother See's daughter Bai laughs self-consciously at the idea of a women's group. She knows there are women's groups in other villages and that the government encourages their formation. But, so far, there is no group in Som Hong. Bai sits at her loom weaving a silk sarong to wear while working in the rice fields. In a few weeks, the entire village will move to the fields they own 20 kilometres away. They will spend a month there living in little huts and planting rice before returning to work the fields around the village where the rains later come. Bai is hurrying to finish her sarong before the planting season begins. She raised the silkworms herself, boiled the cocoons to kill the worms and soften the silk, spun the thread and dyed them – away from the sight of pregnant and menstruating women who are forbidden to watch or take part in the dyeing process. The pattern of the sarong is dyed into the threads that form the weft so that as the shuttle is passed back and forth each bit of colour is where it should be and the design seems magically to grow by itself. Glowing in red and gold and a deep mulberry, the pattern of Bai's sarong is called *Lai Hua Jai Wang* ("The Free Heart").

Bai is one of the best weavers in a village where every woman weaves. But she only began to concentrate on perfecting her technique after her daughter was born. "I want my daughter to learn to weave," she says simply, "so I must also know." Bai's daughter, like most of the other daughters of the village, will attend the village primary school for only four to six years. She will learn to read and write, but later she will probably forget everything except how to sign her name. What she learns from her mother will not be forgotten, however: how to weave, how to cook, how to farm. Unless she decides to join the Bangkok-bound throng, she will marry and spend her entire life in Som Hong or a village nearby, farming in the rainy season and weaving in the dry.

Village boys, on the other hand, have opportunities for education and experience that the girls do not. Those without financial resources to enter the high schools and colleges of the towns can continue their studies in the monkhood, withdrawing later if they wish to resume a secular life. The many young men drafted to serve a term in the army also receive some education and a chance to see the world. For at least the foreseeable future, the monkhood and the army are closed to women. But women's responsibility for the home and children restricts their participation even in those experiences that might be offered to them. Seminars and study tours are largely male affairs, not only because the village leaders are men but because women often cannot take the time off from their families to attend a course. As a result, the worldview of the village women is circumscribed and limited to the small world that they know. They have little chance to learn about the experiences of other women or to consider what relevance a women's group might have in their own lives.

A programme of participatory development implies that people participate because they have realized that their needs can best be addressed through co-operative efforts. The women of Som Hong will not organize a group until the need and the benefits are clear. Many government-sponsored women's groups have dwindled away because the women were either not prepared to form a group, or were not properly supported after the group was officially in existence. In Don Muai, another village in which GRID is operating, the Department of Agriculture taught the women to make fish sauce, but the group dissolved soon after the government lessons were over. No one was interested in making fish sauce because it was too complicated and they preferred to purchase a commercial brand. With the encouragement of the GRID VDA the women have again come together, this time to attempt a collective weaving project, but they have not yet decided what to do with their profits. The Sawal Dod women's group has not met again since distributing the profits of their weaving project among the members.

"I've never sold a sarong," says Bai. "I wouldn't know what price to ask for."

"Two hundred baht," her husband suggests as he picks up his gun and goes out the gate towards the field.

From purchasing the silkworms to the day the sarong is finished it may take an entire year; in Surin, a sarong like this would cost 500 baht or more. Bai thinks about the money, stroking the shining cloth with her hand.

"No one in the village has ever sold a sarong," she says softly.

The women of Som Hong may not be interested in starting a weaving group but another activity may spark their imaginations. The needs of the community are urgent. Women should also be challenged to join forces in combating hunger, debt and dependency, tackling issues of direct concern to them and which, at least in the beginning, do not require them to step too far outside the circle of the home and their immediate community.

A few months ago, Bai and nine other villagers went to visit a herbal-medicine club in Kut Chum district to learn about the culture and usage of medicinal herbs. The nearest health station is several kilometres away, Bai explains, and the nearest hospital is in the town of Kaset Wisai. Often the villagers have neither the time nor the money to seek out health care, especially for minor complaints. Many are addicted to pain-killing powders such as Tamjai, which give them the strength to carry on despite the chronic backaches that come from having stooped for too many years in the rice fields. Now Bai's garden contains a plant that will soothe sore backs as well as Tamjai, without burning ulcers into the stomach lining as Tamjai can do. She also grows aloe for burns and a herbal medicine for chickens, which are not vaccinated in Som Hong and whose raw necks and chests and hideous bulbous growths attest to their need for some form of medical attention. Several of the women are interested in growing herbs and perhaps a women's group could be organized around the promotion and production of herbal medicines. Possibly, as in Ban Plakoon, the women could make capsules of herbal medicines for sale.

A mother–child health programme might provide the needed impetus. An estimated 50 per cent of children in Thung Kula Ronghai suffer from first-degree malnutrition. This condition does not produce the blatant physical symptoms of more serious degrees of malnutrition and thus most mothers are unaware that their children are suffering irreversible damage to their growing bodies and minds. But could such an awareness be created, a women's group might be formed around their concern for their families' health and nutrition. A basic health programme could be started in the village to ensure that children are weighed and vaccinated. Women might raise chickens or cultivate vegetables together to provide nutritious food for their children.

Whatever form the Som Hong women's group may eventually take, within the shelter of this group leadership qualities can be developed and the women's knowledge and awareness broadened to the point where they can decide for themselves if they wish to take a more active role in village affairs and, if so, how they will go about it.

"Ma du kwun oy!"

It is Niang's wedding day and she sits on the floor beside Promah, the man who is almost her husband, looking at her own hands as her uncle calls for the spirits (the *kwun*) to return from their wanderings and take their places in the people sitting within the circle of the sacred string. It is only a few minutes since Promah arrived with his parents and relatives to find the gateway to his bride's home barred with a silver belt. Only after many entreaties and the delivery of a bottle of rice whisky, was the party allowed inside the yard. Niang's mother dressed Promah in a silk sarong and his feet were washed as he stood on a banana leaf laid upon a stone. This was so that he would be calm and clear as he went up to take his bride. Promah has given Niang's parents 9,000 baht – the price of her mother's milk – and, as is the custom, the newly-wed couple will live with her family until they can build their own home. As the spirit doctor finishes his invocation, Niang and Promah extend their hands, and friends and relatives crowd about them to tie more lucky strings around wrists already heavy with wishes. Niang's friends set up a cloth cradle in her room and rock a pillow baby, then dance exuberantly until the whole house shakes while Niang escapes red-faced to the kitchen.

In another room, the grandmothers are asking about aeroplanes. "Can you see houses from the windows? What about people? Water buffaloes? What do you feel so high above the fields?"

Their grey hair is cut short in the old-fashioned style and one venerable lady has stuck a jasmine flower through her ear lobe. As they talk their hands stray to the baskets of betel-nut, chewing material that never leaves their sides. Should any inconceivable occurrence set these grandmothers aboard a jet those baskets would accompany them, firmly clenched in one hand, and vivid patches of betel juice would soon blossom on the broadloom. It is, however, a more likely destiny that one by one the grandmothers will die and their dry remains will burn briefly on a pyre made in their own fields on a sunny afternoon. Not one of them will ever know a moment's regret over not having been a member of the Village

Committee, not one will feel that her opinions were less influential for having been expressed within the home. The grandmothers have wielded power in their time in their own way. But the world is not as it was when they worked beside their husbands to clear the thick forests of Som Hong. And even if Niang herself never cares to state her opinions at a meeting or stand for election in the village or travel to town to negotiate a loan with a government official, the daughter who will soon replace the pillows in the wildly swinging cradle may well grow up to see such participation not only as her right but as her duty.

PIRD in the context of GRID

Recent years have seen the growth of a new approach to development: Participatory Integrated Rural Development (PIRD). PIRD recognizes that village society, composed of different groups with conflicting interests and priorities, is generally far from homogeneous. Therefore, this development approach focuses upon the poorest and most exploited of village members. Due to deep-seated dependency attitudes, the intervention of an agent of change is required to set this process of self-reliant development in motion. Through the methodology of participatory action research (PAR), target groups develop an awareness of the forces behind the socio-economic reality of their poverty and dependence, and their energy and resources are mobilized in a programme of collective action for social change. The people themselves decide on the initiatives and actions they wish to take and maintain control over the project activities.

In South Asia and Latin America, where most of the PIRD programmes have taken place and from whence comes most of the literature on the subject, these activities are frequently of a confrontational kind – strikes, rallies, and the organization of militant unions. In the NET and

GRID programmes in North-East Thailand however, while PAR strategy of conscientization-action-reflection remains the same, the activities through which PIRD manifests itself are largely non-confrontational, reflecting the very different nature of Thai culture and rural society.

South Asian villages tend to be highly stratified. Large numbers of landless labourers are locked into dependency relationships with land-owners and money-lenders. Caste, religion and gender introduce further contradictions. In contrast, while many North-Eastern Thai farmers are unable to produce enough rice to feed their families, few are actually landless and there is a corresponding lack of large land-owners. Questions of caste and religion do not arise in this almost completely Buddhist society, and women enjoy a level of equality found in few other Asian countries.

PIRD in the context of GRID varies from the conventional understanding of the term in its realization that North-Eastern Thai villages are, in fact, largely homogeneous; villagers are seldom in exploitative relationships with one another. Each family manages on its own, though some assistance (such as loans and help with the harvest) is given and received within a loose-knit kinship group. The money-lenders and large rice-mill owners, who are the main human agents assisting the poor along the downward spiral of ever-increasing poverty, generally live in the towns and are not part of village society.

While GRID has in fact chosen a target group – subsistence farmers – it is possible in North-Eastern Thailand to work with villages as a whole, developing village leadership with the assurance that all the villagers who wish to can benefit from the programme.

The strategies developed by the villagers to confront their problems of food shortages and debt, concentrate on increasing village self-sufficiency and self-reliance so that contacts with exploitative outsiders can be reduced. Rather than attempting to pressure money-lenders into lowering their rates, for example, village-based sources of low-cost credit such as rice banks are instituted. Such activities, it has been noted, generally have the effect of forcing the money-lenders in the area to make their rates more competitive, thus improving conditions in surrounding villages as well.

Similarly, when dealing with the government, non-confrontational methods appear to be most effective. In most cases, the major constraints are the villagers' lack of awareness of the availability of government assistance and services and their natural reluctance to have any dealings with remote and "superior" government officials. Government services are theoretically there for the people's benefit but often do not reach them, and therefore the NET and GRID projects aim at developing the villagers' confidence and ability to approach officials and apply for needed assistance.

8.   It Happened in Si Phon Thong Village

by Amporn Kaewnoo of GRID and Kosol Suthangkool

Si Phon Thong is one of the villages in the area of Grass Roots Integrated Development's (GRID's) operations. From 1985 to 1987 Kosol Suthangkool was one of the village workers of GRID in that village. His job had been to help the villagers work out for themselves what they want to do, and then help them to do it. This chapter is the script of a slide/sound show that Kosol and Amporn Kaewnoo made when Kosol was about to leave the village after three years' work there. They showed it to the villagers as a way of reflecting on the developments, both good and bad, that they had seen while working there.

Building a village

The original home of the grandmothers and grandfathers of Si Phon Thong was on the bank of the Siaw River. It was called Ban Toan in Den Lat Sub-District, Phanom Phrai District of Roi Et Province.

Every year, in the flood season, water from the Siaw River came up and submerged the village causing a great deal of difficulty for the villagers. At the same time, the population grew and the village became rather crowded. Land was becoming scarce. It was time to move to a new site.

Scouts were sent to look for a suitable site in the

The Imbalance Between Town and Country

Source: from the village training materials of Proshika MUK,
a Bangladesh NGO, 1985.

Weeping Prairie. The area near Nong Sim swamp was
chosen. The swamp now lies in front of the village school.

Three families constituted the original settlers: Grandfather Phim's, Grandfather Chiangton's and Grandfather
In's. That was 70 or 80 years ago. Nong Sim area then was
plentiful with forest and wild animals such as deer, tigers,
rabbits, wild boars and even foxes. Grandfathers and
grandmothers cut down the forests, cleared the land, grew

rice and other crops. Children and grandchildren kept arriving until today.

In those days, farmers relied on buffaloes for ploughing the fields. No hired hand was needed. Whatever was needed, to eat or use, was made in the households. Cash was not often needed and people were not in debt to outsiders. The villagers led reasonably comfortable lives. If the harvest failed in any year due to floods, they would go fishing in the Mun River. A caravan would be organized to go to other villages and barter fish with rice.

About 60 years ago, Grandfather Chamlun was appointed first headman of the village. He was a son-in-law of Grandfather Phim who was one of the first settlers.

When the village expanded a little more, Grandfather Bunma persuaded the villagers to build a temple for their own spiritual well-being.

In 1940, Phon Thong School was established for the young to study in.

After Headman Chamlun died, Headman Bunmi Sisalai succeeded him. The next one was Headman Noi who was the first elected by the villagers. When Headman Noi retired, Headman Phong succeeded him. In 1980 the village became much bigger and Si Phon Thong emerged from the original Phon Thong Village, headed by Mr Supharp.

Changes

Si Phon Thong, 60 or 70 years ago, used to be plentifully endowed by nature. People did not often undergo hardship. As years passed by, nature suffered badly. The soil was becoming infertile and yields were decreasing. Some villagers tried using chemical fertilizer bought from Sam Kha Village in their fields. The effect was good so others followed suit. Since then, over 20 years ago, Si Phon Thong villagers have become dependent on fertilizer from the market.

The use of chemical fertilizer increased when the Bank of Agriculture and Agricultural Co-operatives (BAAC) entered the rural scene. In succession came the use of pesticides and annual loans from the BAAC, complemented by loans from money-lenders. The villages have been debtors to outsiders from then on.

Accompanying the extensive use of chemical fertilizer is the change of rice varieties over to the Fragrant Rice Variety which was bought from Ban Mao and Song Chan Villages in Suwannaphum District where the government was promoting it. Not much longer afterward, single-axle tractors or "iron buffaloes" (with which you cannot use the dung as manure) began to replace the ones with which you can. Motorized carts replaced cattle-drawn carts. All these novelties cost money and the villagers paid for them by producing more paddy specifically for sale in order to obtain cash to repay loans.

Instead of growing rice for their own consumption as in the past, the villagers now grow it for the rice dealers, fertilizer dealers and medicine dealers. Since there is never enough cash around, life seems not as comfortable as it could be.

As the roads have become more accessible and convenient, all kinds of goods have become available: things to eat and to use in the household; and things for agricultural purposes. Since electricity came to the village in 1985, there is much more comfort to be had and enjoyed. But modernity has to be bought with cash. Goods cannot be bartered like before. More modern goods in the village means more money draining from the village to outside.

Everything has to be bought

In the past, when markets were far away, all kinds of vegetables were grown around the house, and fish and crabs were caught from the fields. Nowadays, food is bought from the market. Each household pays US$ 139.40 each year for it. Another US$46 per household each year is spent on clothes and accessories. Wood used to be gathered from the forest to build houses. No more of that. Now each household pays US$ 160.56 each year for construction materials. More potent modern medicines and doctors are replacing herbs and each household pays an average of US$ 53 each year for these. US$ 43.80 is spent each year for their children to go to school. For pleasure, US$ 16.72 is spent on movies and theatres each year.

In agriculture, cash is also spent to hire labour for ploughing the fields, for transplanting seedlings, to buy fertilizer and pesticides, and to hire others to help in harvesting rice and carrying it.

Altogether, annual household and agricultural expenditures come to an average of US$ 933.52 per household. For the whole village, the total amount is as much as US$ 48,543.56 – a great deal of money.

Meanwhile, an average annual income is only US$ 795.28 per household which means that each household spends US$ 140.64 more that they actually have per year. To pay for this, of course, one has to go into debt. Asking around, it is found that eight out of ten villagers in Si Phon Thong are in debt to the BAAC, a co-operative, village funds, neighbours and merchants. The other two out of ten who are not in debt are either rich or too poor to borrow money. During last year, the total debt in the village amounted to US$ 9,684.60. On average, each household carried a debt burden of US$ 230.56.

Apart from the expenses mentioned, they also get into debt when they buy things on instalment, such as mosquito nets, motorized carts, "iron buffaloes", motorcycles and household equipment.

Too many expenses and too little income has forced the villagers to try to find extra work in Bangkok. They drive taxis, tricycles, and do other jobs. Some go to other provinces to work on sugar-cane plantations. Last year, 79 people went to look for jobs outside the village. They brought back a total of US$ 13,300.80, even more than what the village earned from the sale of rice. But it still did not help decrease the debt burden. What else can be done?

We must help each other

When we have problems or difficulties, we have to help each other. Has the savings fund been helping us? Or is it just a new source of high-interest loans with dwindling membership?

Together we established a co-operative store which sells goods at reasonable prices. Can anything be improved so that all of us can benefit from it fully? We established a bank of rice to help each other, especially those who are in need. How much help has the rice bank been? Have the members assisted the committee? Apart from the problem of making ends meet, what other problems do we face everyday? For example, we still lack drinking water and a domestic water supply.

Ducks and chickens fall prey to diseases. Sometimes there is no water for agriculture if the rain does not fall according to the season. The soil is saline. We lack firewood for fuel. Sometimes, there are quarrels in the village. Some young people are addicted to paint-thinner and this fact may be linked to petty thieving.

Si Phon Thong has prospered a great deal since the old days. Does it not make one wonder why people have become less friendly and less generous toward each other? Si Phon Thong seems to have changed in more ways than we had thought. What are we going to do with the debt burden that keeps multiplying itself? What can we do about all the expenses? Or the loss on the sale of paddy? Or the wastage from poultry disease? How can the savings fund, the co-operative store, the rice bank and the health cards be developed further to help us solve these problems.? Can we co-operate better, avoid conflicts and help each other more? How can our village stand on its own two feet and become more self-reliant?

Let us find the answers together and work on them so as to ensure that Si Phon Thong will be a better home for our children and grandchildren within this wide prairie.

Consolidating Farmers' Knowledge

"No sir, it isn't the Japanese or Chinese or Russian method of cultivation – I tried just plain cultivation and it worked!"

Source: Cartoon by R.K. Laxman in *New Internationalist*, May 1981; originally published in *The Times of India*.

9. From Rice/Fish to Integrated Farming: Sustainable Agriculture for Resource-Poor Farmers in North-East Thailand

by Janet Durno

> Chillies lie in a home north of here;
> Salt lies in the southern home;
> Water morning glory lies awaiting;
> Preserved fish can be found yonder;
> For the asking it will be in your jar.

So go the words of an old North-Eastern Thai saying, reflecting an abundance and a community self-reliance that are now threatened at every turn.

The headman of Klong Namsab village leads the way through fields of newly planted jute past the little house that enshrines the protective spirits of the village, their images roughly scratched on rocks.

"The name of this village means 'Place of Ever-Present Water,' " the headman remarks bitterly as he arrives at a dry stream-bed set in a quiet, eerie landscape of grassy hillocks and the burnt stumps of what were once giant trees. Far away on a hillside, small figures move over a ploughed field in the grey evening light, planting peanuts.

Klong Namsab, founded perhaps 20 years ago, is not an old village. The headman was one of the first to arrive, migrating from Ubon province where he had been struggling to raise ten children on only three rai (2.5 rai equals 1 acres; 6.2 rai equals 1 hectare) of land. He hired himself out as a labourer, falling more deeply into debt every year.

When he heard that there was land for the clearing in Surin he did not hesitate to move, despite the malaria that infested the forest, and despite the fact that the forest was government property and he might never have a legal deed to his land. With his family he cleared 70 rai.

"But we still cannot grow enough," he says. "The family is so big and the land is so poor. Every year we must buy many sacks of rice to eat."

Further up the stream there is still some water. The headman squats beside the pool and lifts up a fishing net that has been suspended there for hours. It is empty. He lets it fall back into the water. Now that the forest is gone the stream no longer runs all year.

"In the past we had fish. We grew vegetables on the banks of the stream. Now there is nothing here."

The old people in the villages of Surin province can still remember a time when much of the North-East was mantled in a thick forest which provided for many of their needs – animals to kill for meat, wild vegetables and fruit, wood for houses and fuel. The villagers, who could combine rice growing with a hunting/gathering lifestyle to obtain most of their needs, were far from rich but they were largely self-sufficient. Today the North-East, which constitutes one-third of Thailand in both area and population, is the least developed part of the country, with the majority of its 16 million people rice farmers who exist at subsistence level.

Though much of the region is still officially registered as virgin forest, the great trees have been logged and the land taken over by a growing population desperate for farms. With the deforestation of critical watersheds, the water resources have become unreliable and the climate unpredictable. Drought may sear the rice crop at the beginning of the season; floods may drown it at the end. The sandy, saline, infertile soils produce little rice, as low as half a tonne per hectare.

The land of the North-East is inhospitable enough and its people poor enough that so far they have been spared much of the pressure to implement a "green revolution" and other "modern" agricultural systems. There are few large land-owners, little irrigation infrastructure, and little incentive to invest in expensive packages of chemical inputs. The yields from the depleted soils are so low that even a 50 per cent increase in crop yield is almost never profitable if chemicals must be purchased to obtain this growth. Nevertheless, convinced that chemical fertilizers are their only hope of realizing an adequate yield, every year farmers take out loans to purchase as much as they can – at crippling annual interest rates that may run to 100 or 150 per cent.

At harvest time, 20 per cent of a villager's crop may go to pay back the interest on his loan. So much of the crop is sold that the villagers face rice shortages for an average of 143 days a year. Even before the planting season arrives, many villagers have run out of rice. Now not only must they borrow once again to buy fertilizer, they must also buy rice, at inflated prices, to feed their families until the next harvest. Debts are also incurred when a family cere-mony – a wedding or the ordination of a monk – must be celebrated in the proper style; or when a serious illness or death occurs. The money-lenders are patient. Debts accumulate from year to year and are passed on to the next generation. To understand the North-East one must realize that, while many North-Eastern communities lack basic facilities such as health services, electricity and all-weather roads, the interlocking issues of food shortages and heavy debt are of overriding importance.

Lacking the forest products which once supplemented their rice production or acted as a buffer during hard times, life for the farmers of the North-East has become a struggle to provide adequately for their families, and reliance on commercial goods has increased. Foodstuffs that could once be gathered from the land and necessities that were once produced within the village are now being bought from travelling merchants or in the markets of the towns. With improved communications and transportation, the villagers – no longer as isolated as before – are facing the transition from a closed, rural, subsistence economy to one influenced by money, market forces and the urban culture of the towns. With a growing interest in modern ways the villagers come to denigrate or dismiss their traditional knowledge and skills. Later, when "modern" technologies or methods prove inappropriate, the indigenous solutions may already have been lost. Farmers traditionally grow many varieties of rice, for example, choosing the best type for each patch of land – the wet field, the dry field, the field with a certain kind of soil. Thus, despite the droughts and floods and pest attacks, some of the rice varieties should survive and bear a crop. But with the push towards monocultures of high-yielding rice varieties, the protection of traditional diversity is lost. If a pest attacks it can wipe out the entire crop. Farmers may then attempt to return to a tried and true traditional rice variety only to find that it no longer exists.

Nevertheless, the modern world continues to impinge ever more closely on the villages. New expectations and demands have been created while the ability to meet these demands has lagged far behind. Manufactured goods, services and modern technologies come with a high price tag, especially for those who live far away from the market towns, while the world is witnessing a sharp drop in the prices of those very commodities, such as rice and jute, upon which the villagers depend for their income. Often there is in any case little surplus of commodities for sale or barter. It may be argued that the villagers should attempt to grow more cash crops for sale, but a reliance on cash crops leaves a villager at the mercy of the uncertainties of the world market, while there is little enough land even to grow the food needed for basic subsistence. Nevertheless a cash economy has come to the villages and money must be got from somewhere.

Migration is not a new phenomenon in Thailand. For the past several decades farmers from all over the country – especially from the poorest regions of the North and North-East – have left their farms and families for several months each year, between the harvest and the beginning of the next planting season, to seek out paid employment in the towns. Whether they drive taxis, work on construction sites, or harvest sugar cane, the hours are long and the pay is low. Nevertheless, in a short time a man can amass what is, in village terms, a good sum of money. For many the alternation of farming and migration has become a way of life.

However, the migration pattern is changing. Now it is often the young people of the villages who leave, compelled by a desire to contribute income to their families and an eagerness to experience the delights of an urban life they may have seen in a movie or on the televisions that came with electricity into the villages. Searching for jobs in factories or the entertainment industry, these young people swell the cheap labour pool in Bangkok and the larger towns. In 1978 it was reported that there were over a million children aged 11 to 14 on the labour market, 32 per cent working more than 13 hours a day, 52 per cent working without holidays. Despite abysmal conditions and low pay, many see more opportunities in the cities than on the land and will never return to their villages to stay. There are also many casualties: well over half of the estimated one million Thai prostitutes are girls under 16.

Some of the North-Eastern farmers are so entangled in their desperate lives that they see no way out and give up trying to find one. But the majority are amazingly resourceful and courageous, struggling against great odds to make a decent living from their land. These farmers are working to reduce their need to purchase inputs in order to reduce their costs, while still maintaining or increasing yields. Many are developing sustainable systems of farming which make maximum use of all available resources, recreating on the farm a diverse and stable natural environment with all its complex inter-relationships and inter-dependencies.

Such farmers do not depend on the availability of outside advice and assistance, which so often come to the villages with packages of expensive technologies and inputs in hand. Instead, farmers start with their own indigenous knowledge and practices and, with the resources available to them, learn and teach by example. One such local initiative, which is spreading rapidly and spontaneously among farmers in the North-East, is rice/fish cultivation.

The rice fields that cover most of the lowland areas of Thailand provide a natural habitat for fish during the rainy season when the fields are flooded. Entering the fields from overflowing ponds and streams, these fish provide the farmer with a bonus crop to be caught as the family has need of them, with any remaining fish harvested along with the rice. But the wild fish that were once abundant in streams and ponds have diminished along with the water and few fish are now to be found in the fields. Fish have always been a staple item in the Thai diet and the major source of protein. Poor farming families are suffering from this drop in protein consumption; in some areas over 50 per cent of pre-school children suffer from malnutrition and the shortage of nutritious food also affects the health and energy of adults.

The fish that are reappearing in the fields of North-East Thailand are no longer wild but rather are introduced cultured varieties, fish that are suitable both for home consumption and for sale. A few years ago only a few enterprising farmers were experimenting with rice/fish but now hundreds are following their example. A number of organizations, both foreign (the International Development Research Centre) and local (the Farming Systems Research Institute and the Appropriate Technology Association), have begun to mobilize support for farmers' efforts and for on-farm research into the variety of rice/fish culture methods. However, the true impetus for the development and spread of rice/fish farming lies with the farmers themselves.

While rice/fish cultivation is a new concept in North-East Thailand, it is not in fact new on the global scene. In China, rice/fish culture can be dated back to the Han dynasty (100 AD) and the technique was probably introduced into south-east Asia 1,500 years ago. Farmers in Central Thailand began using modern rice/fish culture methods in the 1950s but the practice has declined over the past 20 years. With the advent of the green revolution and intensive irrigation, two rice crops a year can now be grown in the Central Plains and the fertilizers and pesticides required by the high yielding varieties (HYVs) of crops have saturated the fields, ruining them for fish. In the poorer North-East, where most farmers grow only one crop of rain-fed rice a year (irrigation covers less than 1 per cent of the region) and cannot afford such large quantities of chemical inputs, the fields have remained relatively uncontaminated.

Rice/fish culture is an extension of Thai farmers' traditional farming and fishing skills and requires few inputs other than labour. As a low-cost, low-risk venture, rice/fish is attractive to small farmers who may have no savings or access to credit and who cannot afford to take chances with their families' already precarious livelihoods. Initially of course, labour demands and costs are greater than in rice only farming, especially in the first year when the fields must be prepared and fingerlings obtained. While management practices vary widely, it is necessary to build higher bunds (raised earth walls) around the rice field to prevent cultured fish from escaping and predators from entering. A nursery pond is needed to rear fish fry and to keep parent fish for breeding. And if there is no natural low spot to provide a retreat when drought lowers the water level in the field, farmers must dig trenches or a refuge for the fish.

But if a farmer uses his own labour to prepare the fields, the purchase of the fingerlings is usually the largest expense he will incur and, with a year-round pond to keep the parent fish, most of the fish fry needed for subsequent seasons can be produced. (Tilapia begin breeding at three months and common carp also spawn with ease.) Other expenses involve the purchase of supplementary fish food, particularly rice bran, but a variety of household wastes and by-products such as manure and tree leaves can also be used.

The fish raised in the fields are tilapia (*Sarotherodon niloticus* and *S.niloticus x mossambicus*), silver barb (*Puntius gononiotus*) and common carp (*Cyprinus carpio*). Unlike wild fish which are for the most part either tiny or carnivorous, these three fast-growing species feed on plants and insects. Each has its own food preference (the silver barb is a surface feeder for example, while the carp prefers bottom detritus) and thus the practice of rearing the fish in a polyculture enables the efficient conversion of weeds, insects and wastes into protein for human consumption. In the four or five months that the rice fields are flooded, some of these fish will attain weights of up to half a kilogram, but even the smallest fish end up in fish sauce or the pungent *pla raa* ("rotten fish") that accompanies almost every North-Eastern meal.

It appears that the presence of fish serves to increase the rice yield while reducing the need for chemical fertilizers, important factors for subsistence farmers at a time when falling rice prices are making the purchase of chemical inputs economically unfeasible. Fish wastes and the extra feed given to the fish – manure, rice bran, termites and vegetables – provide organic fertilizer while the movement of the fish serves to spread the waste material evenly over the field.

Rice/fish makes good sense for a resource-poor farmer: fish and rice by-products are not wasted but rather are used to maximize the production of both. In many cases farmers have found that the rice yield in a rice/fish field is equal to or higher than that of a rice-only field, even when no chemical fertilizer is applied. After the first season the expenses of a rice/fish field are generally lower than those of a rice only field because the farmer needs to purchase fewer chemical inputs. The profitability of an established rice/fish field can actually be double that of an ordinary field, taking into account the higher yield of rice and the sale of fish and fingerlings, which can become an important source of income for the cash-poor farmers.

The fields around Kampua's house are filled with reddish-brown water and the morning sun glints off a thousand ripples. The rice seedlings were transplanted a month ago and are now well enough established that the fish fingerlings can be released into the field. The cultured fish will not be the only inhabitants of the field. There are also wild fish, little darting *siw* (Blue Danio) and a few carnivorous snakehead catfish lurking in the corners. A tiny frog disappears in a shimmering splash while a crab fades silently back into a hole under a rice plant. Dragonflies perch on the landing strips of leaves, a stick insect awaits its prey, a snake slides down the bund towards the water, thinking about an early lunch of fish. A rice field has a complicated ecology all its own and the cultured fish represent a new variable. How do they affect the intricate relationships among predators and prey, most importantly the relationship that exists between insects and rice? Kampua has been raising fish for four years.

"Definitely the fish eat insects," he says. "Crabs are afraid of them and don't want to live in the rice/fish fields. Where there are fish there are always fewer diseases, fewer pests." Ask any rice/fish farmer about fish and pests and his answer will be the same as Kampua's.

The use of chemical pesticides is still quite restricted in the North-East due to the expense and the recognized health hazards. Those who do use pesticides apply them selectively to affected areas of the crop, for example placing balls of pesticide-laced sticky rice beside crab holes. But diseases and pests remain an ever-present menace and the protection provided by the fish is a significant factor in their favour. The fish seem to control many pests and diseases by eating insects, and by feeding on the weeds and phytoplankton that not only compete with the rice for nutrients but may also act as carriers of disease and hosts for pests.

Though it is already July, the rains are reluctant to visit Khon Kaen this year. Ban Fang's pond, where an old lady sits fishing, is half empty. Many of the fields are still mantled in an unploughed pelt of withered grass. The rice plants that a few optimistic farmers have transplanted are ringed with deep dry circles of cracked earth and their vivid leaves are yellowing. On one side of the bund, in the middle of this desolation, dessicated fields stretch away towards the village; on the other side, Noolit crouches in a patch of bright green morning glory – a common vegetable – feeding rice bran to the fish in one of his three ponds.

Noolit began raising fish two years ago. His ponds hold

water all year round so he is able to keep a stock of fish through the dry season and he notes with pride that he will not have to purchase tilapia fingerlings this year, and in fact will be able to give some to his friends because the parent fish have spawned. When the rains finally do come and the water level rises, the fish will leave the pond to forage in the neighbouring rice field.

Fish are not the only creatures that call the ponds their home. Ducks swim noisily in a far corner of one pond and Noolit is raising pigs in a hut built on stilts over another. There is plenty of water for the pigs, and the fish can be seen congregating in the shade of the hut waiting for tasty morsels of manure and feed to fall.

The high banks around Noolit's ponds are planted with many kinds of vegetables and fruit trees: corn, chillies, sugar cane, papaya, banana, cucumbers and beans. Multi-purpose trees such as *neem* and *leucaena* are dotted about the ponds and along the bunds beside the fields. The leaves of some of these trees provide green manures; others contain natural pesticides; and many of the various leaves, flowers and fruits are nutritious foods for people, animals and fish. The random and diverse nature of the plantings is typical of the mixed tree/herb gardens that still surround village houses, where native varieties of plants thrive on shade and competition, discouraging the spread of pests and partitioning the resources of water, sunlight and nitrogen far more efficiently than plants grown in a mono-culture. Such gardens, too, yield a continuous supply of foodstuffs which can be harvested as needed on a daily basis, rather than following a cycle of glut and dearth.

Water is the critical factor limiting agriculture in the North-East. While the rainfall is adequate (100 cm per year) it is erratic and the sandy laterite soils do not retain water well. Rice/fish culture encourages, indeed requires, the development of the small-scale water resources such as ponds which are the key to the adoption of integrated, sustainable agricultural systems. Many of the "water-rich" rice/fish farmers go on, like Noolit, to add new practices to their farming systems, in a sense transforming themselves from rice-growers to agriculturalists. Suddenly these farmers are producing the meat, vegetables, fruits and fish that they can no longer harvest from the natural environment. Nutrition is improved, and any surplus of these commodities can be sold for a much higher profit than rice. Some farmers are beginning to experiment with raising vegetables or fish instead of rice in a field and may find it to be far more profitable.

In some parts of the North-East, the interest in sustainable agriculture systems has been set within the context of Participatory Integrated Rural Development (PIRD) programmes implemented by Thai NGOs. Development workers, or *animateurs*, work with the people to identify village leaders and encourage the formation of village co-operatives through which the people can address their problems and needs. In such PIRD programmes, the villagers' traditional knowledge, skills and customs are highly valued and form the basis for village-level solutions to the ever-present spectres of hunger and debt. On the individual level, this will involve the maximization of food production while reducing the need for expensive agricultural inputs. This can be achieved through the adoption of such practices as rice/fish culture; the use of green manures and compost; and through a return to traditional methods of integrated pest control. With a growing sense of self-reliance on their own farms and a pride in the efficacy of the old ways, the villagers can turn their co-operative traditions – building houses together, reciprocal labour at harvest time – to new uses.

In Som Hong village, fish-raising is not only an individual pursuit. The entire community has co-operated this year in preparing a pond to raise fish collectively, using the money that was donated to the *wat* (the Buddhist temple) by villagers working in Bangkok. An old pond beside the lake was enlarged and the people spent a day catching the fish-eating snakes and the large fish that would menace the fingerlings. The Government Fisheries Department was contacted by the Village Committee and assisted with a donation of 20,000 fingerlings. The fish are fed mainly on rice bran which the villagers take turns to scatter on the water, morning and evening, under the watchful supervision of the abbot. A villager himself, the abbot takes a keen interest in agriculture and is often to be seen working in the vegetable plots which surround the sides of the pond, his orange robes glowing among the beans.

When the fish are bigger, they will be released into the lake to continue their growth. The villagers have not yet decided how they will co-ordinate the eventual capture and distribution of the fish but those decisions will be a part of an ongoing process – the growth of community co-operation and self-reliance. Working together, the villagers of Som Hong will be able to stock their lake with fish, a project none of them could have carried out alone and from which all will benefit. Soon, the travelling fish-truck from which the people now purchase most of their fish, trading their small and precious reserves of rice, will be seen no more in Som Hong.

The use of the money traditionally donated to the village temple to facilitate a community fish-raising project is an excellent example of a new use for old customs. In other North-Eastern villages, the rice donated annually to the monks is finding a home in village rice banks. Rice banks and fertilizer funds are innovations directed right at the heart of the vicious circle of indebtedness. In the banks, rice donated by the villagers is stored for future lending at a much lower interest rate than that charged by local money-lenders. The loans are repaid with rice which then augments the bank's store. Some of the village rice banks have progressed to the point where they can function as a marketing tool. As the harvest season approaches, the bank sells off its remaining stock and purchases newly-harvested rice from villagers. Rather than each individual making his own marketing arrangements, the group can offer a large volume of rice to the rice mill. With more bargaining power, a better price can be obtained.

A fertilizer fund involves the villagers in a community debt for which they are all responsible and maximizes the advantage of buying fertilizer in bulk. The Village Committee arranges for a loan, often from an NGO, to buy the fertilizer needed by the village. Each villager repays the loan after the harvest with an agreed amount of rice and the profits after repaying the large loan remain with the fertilizer fund. Several villages are now able to use their community fund to purchase fertilizer without recourse to an outside loan. In some areas, commercial interest rates on fertilizer loans have decreased as merchants have been forced to reduce their rates in order to remain competitive with the fertilizer funds.

Can the long process of empowerment – in agriculture, in the village – begin with a step as seemingly small as deciding to try out a few fish in a rice field? Of course there is far more to it than this but the growth of individual and community dignity, assurance and self-reliance proceeds by a series of small steps. There is more in the villages of North-East Thailand now – more food, more hope, perhaps soon more people if the new opportunities encourage the young people to stay on the land.

The lady in the bright pink sarong has been fishing in the Ban Fang village pond for some time now, alternating between her fishing rod and a big dip net. In her pail she has a handful of tiny wriggling shrimp and a climbing perch one inch long. Fortunately her family's livelihood does not depend on today's catch and so she is smiling and happy as she putters about the pond. But the farmers of Ban Fang cannot feed their families on such meagre fare. No longer able to rely on the bounty of forest and stream, they must work to recreate that bounty on their own small plots of land – recycling resources, wasting nothing, and improving the land through wise and careful use. They must work to recreate community self-reliance, too, joining the village committee, managing revolving funds, seeking out their own creative and appropriate solutions to their own problems. Now once again there can be chillies in the southern home, preserved fish in the jars, and villagers giving to one another for the asking – adding perhaps a small interest payment to be used for the good of all.

10. Partners in Development? The Government and NGOs in Indonesia

by Richard Holloway

This chapter describes the gap between rhetoric and reality in dealing with collaboration between the government and NGOs in Indonesia. It first appeared as an article in *Prisma*, a magazine of the Indonesian NGO LP3ES (the Institute for Education, Information and Socio-Economic Research), in 1984. Richard Holloway is a long-time worker in development and has lived in Indonesia, whose language he speaks.

Development in Indonesia

Remarkable changes have taken place in Indonesia over the last 10 years. Statistics produced by the World Bank (though we may be worried by the distortions implicit in such generalized figures) inform us that: primary-school enrolment has doubled since 1971; infant mortality has declined by 25 per cent since 1969; life expectancy has increased by 6 years since 1969; there are now 2,500 calories available on average to each person per day, compared to 2,097 calories in 1970; adult literacy is now 62 per cent as against 39 per cent in 1960; and GNP (gross national product) per capita is now US$ 530, whereas it was only US$ 100 in 1972. These are no mean achievements. Indonesia has also shown that it can weather a

Blockages in the System

Source: Bulletin Nelayan, a publication of the All Indonesia Fishermen's Association, out of print (1980).

downturn in oil prices and at least one poor harvest (1982) without deep trouble. Few other Third World countries can claim this.[1]

We have seen a huge amount of funds spent on schools, training centres, factories, health centres, hospitals, housing estates, water supply and irrigation projects, fertilizer stores, and rice warehouses. There is no doubt that expenditures on rice, seeds, fertilizers, pesticides, and the programmes to deliver them, have been enormous. Nevertheless, in spite of the statistics, if we look closer we can see that there are still many problems within these huge achievements.

To place the achievements listed above in perspective, however, we know that there is a huge school drop-out rate; that there is a growing problem of unemployment among the young and the educated; that health centres are under-used; that many cannot afford to use hospitals; that drinking-water facilities tend not to last very long; that irrigation mainly helps those with land while the numbers of landless grow; and that the co-operatives that are meant to deliver agricultural inputs have a history of poor performance.[2] There is also increasing evidence of corruption and the misuse of government funds, as large amounts of money are privately pocketed.[3] Furthermore, the estimated number below the poverty line is at least 15 per cent and perhaps as many as 17 per cent (that is 25,000,000 people).[4] Thus, there seems to be a contradiction between what has been attained and the uneven distribution of these achievements, between efforts to implement human development[5] and frequent mismanagement, between the great number of projects realized and the poor performance of many of them.

One way of resolving this contradiction was supplied in 1978 by Karl Jackson when he wrote that, "Corruption is increasing, but because of the existence of slack resources, organisation achievements are multiplying at an even faster rate, and hence the state is progressing, albeit at a less than optimal rate."[6] This used to be true. As long as the price of oil remained high, there were plenty of "slack resources" and the government could try to achieve its development objectives by spending more and more money. This situation is now unlikely to recur and the government will have to do its work with considerably less income. The same impact will have to be achieved with less, and quality rather than quantity will have to be stressed. The 1983 Cabinet's recently proclaimed resolve to reform government machinery can be seen as an attempt to deal with this problem.

Official programmes

A change in methodology from quantity to quality is no easy thing. A methodology encourages quantitative results and the spending of large amounts of money appeals to many aspects of the Indonesian political culture such as the propensity for top-down decision making, the desire for patron–client relationships, and the respect that is considered due to someone exercising the power that money gives them. A methodology that encourages quality will have to cope with other aspects of Indonesian political culture such as the unwillingness of subordinates to report a lack of success to their superiors, and the attention paid to form and public appearances, rather than content and what is actually relevant. The civil-service structure and style of work, described so well by Emmerson, does not easily lend itself to modification in the direction of quality because,

in sum, top-down authority and one-way communication characterize the Indonesian bureaucracy both internally and in relation to the society it administers. Unresponsiveness to social problems among them long-standing inequalities in distribution, and in the concrete circumstances of millions of individual villagers – is a necessary cost of this kind of political and administrative closure.[7]

The structural problems Emmerson notes can also be seen as evidence of the attitudes and assumptions of many civil servants concerning the people who are the target of development and, in particular, the rural poor. These can be summarized as follows:

(i) Government officials think that poor peasants are ignorant and need to be guided. They think that peasants are not capable of judging for themselves what is needed and therefore require advice and guidance from government officials. Government programmes therefore have elaborate rules and regulations to instruct officials who will guide the peasants. These instructions are often designed for administrative convenience rather than to reflect and adapt to the reality of the poor. Lower level officials are often more interested in obeying the rules than in really helping the poor.

(ii) Programmes are designed by planners, that is people whose main job is planning. They live in the main towns and not in the villages. Inputs from people with village experience are rarely heard and rarely sought. If village people do have a chance to speak, often in defence of their superiors, they merely suggest what has already been done, or what they know will be approved.

(iii) Government officials think that the benefits of programmes will "trickle down"; that is, programmes are aimed at middle-level rural peasants in the hope and expectation that the benefits that they receive will spread to the poorer people. The people who implement such programmes are the village authorities who, by definition, are members of the village élite and are quite well off. The desires of these village élites are not always the same as the desires of the village poor. It is too optimistic to believe that village élites will allow or assist help to "trickle down"; they are much more likely to "filter out" any assistance and take the help for themselves.

(iv) Government officials do not seem to recognize the realities of life for the rural poor. The poor are silent; they do not speak in village meetings. They are frightened of officials, and are scared to use officially provided credit, preferring a personal relationship to a patron. They are in debt and cannot afford to antagonize the village officials. They do not join groups outside their immediate circle because they are frightened of being further exploited. They live in villages, and usually the poorer hamlets of those villages, not in the sub-district capitals (*kecamatan*) where so many of the government services are provided.

Increasingly, therefore, large numbers of the poor cannot be aided by government programmes that were, in theory, designed to help them. Someone without land or a boat gets very little advantage from the village co-operative (KUD or KUD/P), while those who have either (or both) receive a lot of advantages and become richer, increasing the gap between rich and poor. In practice, existing farmers' and fishermen's associations represent only those with capital and not with those that own neither land nor boats. A poor man cannot use KIK or KMKP (credit schemes for small-scale investment and permanent working capital) because he has no collateral to show the bank; a poor person does not visit the Community Health Centre (PUSKESMAS) either because it is too far away or because he cannot afford the fee. A poor handicapped person cannot afford to visit the Loka Bina Karya (workshop) in the *kecamatan* capital even though it was designed to help him or her. And it would be too hopeful to expect the Village Community Resilience Institutes (LKMD), which are composed of village élites, to press for a programme to help the landless or to eradicate debt, even though these may be the most serious problems. This is due to the fact that these same élites are themselves exploiting those who need money or land.

Another problem is that government programmes are often designed for large administrative units. No allowances are made for the variety of conditions that exist within districts (*kabupaten*). Some areas are much more needy than others, but government programmes are often applied equally on a geographic basis. This is sometimes defended as equitable distribution but is more like a political trade-off by a governor or District Head (*Bupati*) who wants to hand out equal favours to all his constituencies. The result can be that areas which are already quite well off make use of the programmes and become richer, while the poorer areas may not be able to make efficient use of the programmes at all.

In general, government programmes are based on the belief that villages are unified communities in which all can share equally in the benefits of development as organized by the government. In fact, the bonds of community in the Indonesian village are very strong in many areas – local environment, welfare, emergencies, government administration – but when it comes to raising income, the village no longer remains a unified community. When we talk about making money (and this is what the poorest need most), the villages divides along lines of wealth. Working with village élites is more likely selectively to help the village élites and may even make things worse for the poorest because the village élites will become stronger, ignore their customary responsibilities, demand a larger share of the harvest, and possibly exploit the poorest even further. If we are serious about helping the poorest village members, it is necessary to set up structures which reflect the needs of them alone and which single them out for special attention. If this is not done, the tendency will be for the élites to "filter out" any benefits and for the gaps between them and the poorest to become even larger.

Non-Government programmes

We have looked at the achievements and the shortcomings of government programmes and seen how these derive from civil servants' attitudes, rigid bureaucratic structures and politics. There are, however, other practitioners of development whose experience is relevant and who operate without these shortcomings, although they may well have others. I refer to that wide range of organizations collectively known to British English speakers as NGOs (non-government organizations) and to American English speakers as PVOs (private voluntary organizations). There are many of these in Indonesia, ranging from Jakarta-based national organizations working in many provinces, to small bodies limited to one village. In comparison with the scope of the government's programmes, they are tiny. In terms of the number of people they affect in the context of Indonesia's total population, they are marginal. However, they can be pioneers with the flexibility to try out ideas that the government would never attempt on its own. Often, if government has not blocked these ideas it subsequently picks them up and tries to incorporate them into its own programmes. The NGOs' way of working, however, differs from that of the government in many respects:

(i) Their main strength is the high level of commitment of their staff (and in particular their fieldworkers) who have a strong identification with the problems of the poor and a strong commitment to doing something about it.

(ii) NGOs are not usually very hierarchical. They encourage suggestions from the field and decisions are often taken at field level. Since they do not have a "party line" to follow they are prepared to report on the reality of what they see in villages and work with it, even if it is different from the accepted view.

(iii) They are usually limited in their coverage and scope. They do not try to cover large areas, or to replicate projects very widely and are able to put a lot of human resources into relatively small projects.

(iv) They work out their own priorities in accordance with their own perception of needs. This enables them to do things which the government has not thought of, or things which the government has not yet focused on.

(v) They can work out their own channels for reaching the poorest. Within the broad framework of the culture and organization of the village, they are able to devise new structures and methods of work.

The following are some examples of NGO programmes to help the poorest which show this flexibility:

(i) One way is to search for traditional social structures that are not imposed from above, or dominated by élites, and to use them as a basis for helping the poor. One such example is the *arisan*.[8] With skilled management, such groups can become the basis for credit unions and pre-co-operatives that will selectively help the poorer people in the village to save their money, borrow from each other, develop their capacity to escape exploitation from the money-lender and to help themselves. This approach has been used for many years by Bina Swadaya.

(ii) Another way is to modify existing programmes that

are purely charitable so that they become more oriented towards helping people to become self-reliant. Many Mohammadiyah groups have been giving out food and money to the poor for years at the end of the fasting month, without reducing the numbers of the poor. Now some Mohammadiyah groups see the value of using the same structure to help less people more intensively so that they can become self-sufficient and escape from their poverty.

(iii) Another is to use new structures created by the government and to expand their role, often to involve income-producing activities. PPM Dhorowati from Yogyakarta has worked with the Family Welfare Education (PPK) movement to introduce them to collective enterprises. Bina Swadaya, at the invitation of the National Family Planning Coordination Board (BKKBN), have started to work with groups of people who come to them for contraception, making these people a starting point for income-generating projects.

(iv) A fourth way is to select the poorest for special help. I know of only two government programmes which do this – the Assistance for Poor Families Programme (Bantuan Keluarga Miskin) of the Department of Social Affairs, and the Programme to Increase Poor Peasants' Incomes (P4K) of the Department of Agriculture. Both have experienced difficulties adapting the civil-service methodology to this new approach. The Indonesian Church in Klampok Banjarnegara and CD Bethesda in Yogyakarta DIY have, however, been targeting their work in this way for many years. If an income-generation programme is offered to a village as a whole it will quickly be absorbed by the village élites. If, however, the *Lurah* (village head), as the father of his people, is asked to select the 30 poorest people in his village for special treatment, it is very likely that he will approach this work in a different spirit and will indeed select the poorest who can then be helped selectively, usually with small loans, which will help them to become self-supporting.

An element common to many NGO programmes is the attempt to utilize the resources that the people already have, even though these may be very small, rather than dropping assistance on them for which they have not been prepared. It is naïve, however, to expect the government and NGOs to look objectively at each other's programmes as fellow practitioners of development. There is a background of emotion and suspicion from both sides which clouds the ability to appreciate the most relevant and efficient programmes. To see why this has happened it is necessary to look at the nature of the relationship between the Government and NGOs in Indonesia and their mutual expectations.

Differences between the Government and NGOs

In all Third World countries, the definition of "development" is made by the government. With differing degrees of efficiency, the government states the aims, makes the policy and sets the pace. It then frequently requests assistance from friendly states or from the United Nations (UN) to enable its idea of development to be carried out. Many countries, however, recognize that "development" as defined by the government is not exclusive – that there are bodies other than government which have a useful contribution to make to the development of that country and that the government does not have a monopoly on ideas, policy or practice. So long as these bodies supplement or complement the government's programmes, and do not actively oppose them, they are tolerated and allowed to seek funds from friendly states. There is a spectrum of attitudes that range from allowing only the state to be involved in development to tolerating anybody trying their hand. Burma is an example of the extreme where only the state can carry out development projects whereas India is a country where most development groups are tolerated.

Each position has its proponents and its detractors. Opponents of monolithic government control over development usually say that it is inflexible, unwieldy, and difficult to adapt to new circumstances; that it involves the people only as the objects of centrally designed programmes and is liable to become fossilized and corrupt. Opponents of non-government bodies involved in development usually talk specifically about their political challenge to authority or else they talk disparagingly of their marginality and unimportance, their *ad hoc*, piecemeal, unplanned and finally ineffective approaches, and their frequent changes in policy. Many of these accusations are justified, but we have only to think of the Sarvodaya movement in Sri Lanka, or the Gandhian movement in India, or the Red Cross/Red Crescent in many countries to be shown that significant development can be achieved by non-government groups.

Most Third World countries have, to a greater or lesser degree, a mixture of both government and non-government resources devoted to the development process, and Indonesia is no exception. As in many other Third World countries, the government in Indonesia has no competitors at the macro level, in large physical infrastructure and communications projects (except perhaps the industrial enclaves like Freeport, Irian Jaya, where those involved in private enterprise virtually run a state within a state and control their own infrastructure). The government is not, however, the only initiator of ideas and practitioner in fields that deal directly with people at the micro level. Examples of these are education, saving, welfare, health, extension services and co-operatives, as well as more locally based small-scale infrastructure such as local roads, drinking water and irrigation. To talk of competition at the macro level is absurd – NGO activities are tiny when compared with the governments' – but NGOs not infrequently have the edge in quality at the micro level and show an ability to be innovative, to involve the participation of the people, and to be responsive to local conditions in a way that often contrasts with government efforts.

In the New Order period since the overthrow of Sukarno in 1965, the Indonesian government has devoted a lot of effort to ensuring state security, complete loyalty to the official state philosophy of *Pancasila* (particularly the civil servants) and to avoiding the chaos of the Old Order. For these reasons, NGOs whose origins have often been religious groups (Muslim, Catholic or Protestant) have, until recently, been seen mostly as potentially destabilizing political forces. The government has been particularly worried about groups of village-level organizations whose development activities might mask political agitation. This concern came to a head in 1972 when the various political parties were reduced to three (Golkar, PPP, PDI). In the following year, a large number of fishermen's, farmers' and workers' organizations were subsumed into the government-controlled HNSI, HKTI and FBSI (fishermen's, peasants' and workers' organizations).

Since that time, there have been further attempts by the government to replace NGO networks with those of their own, although this has been voluntary rather than by decree. Examples are GUPPI for the Pesantren, KUDs for the farmers' co-operatives, and BKKBN for the Family Planning Association of Indonesia (PKBI). In addition, the gradual expansion of government departments has, in many places, taken over work previously done in part by the NGOs. This has been particularly true of the Outer Islands where recently government services have rapidly expanded. Sometimes there has been a "live and let live" philosophy and sometimes government has tried to bring NGO activities under their own control such as in the case of the SFMA (Farming Schools) of Central Java, and various co-operatives. The strength of the desire to control NGO activities often depends on the personality of the civil servant in place at the time.

Over the past 10 years, however, the government has come to realize, particularly at higher, national levels, that the experiences and capabilities of NGOs are valuable, that they are not necessarily subversive, and that government programmes can learn from them. (In the absence of any national policy statement to this effect, however, provincial and *kabupaten* officials more frequently maintain the previous attitude of suspicion and the desire to control). At the same time, there is a realization that some government programmes have failed to achieve their objectives and have sometimes failed to extend their benefits to the large mass of the poor.

Indonesia has often expanded its human-development activities through aid. With aid comes advisers and they, often frustrated by the inflexibility of the government machinery, have turned to Indonesian NGOs for fresh ideas and experiences. There are now new elements at high levels of the Indonesian government who recognize the value of NGOs, particularly their skills in eliciting people's participation and in training others in these methods. With the end of the high oil prices which enabled the government to pay for more and more projects, successful or otherwise, people's participation will become increasingly important in Indonesian government programmes that operate at the village level. The government will no longer have the seemingly endless resources to "drop" projects on villages whether or not they want them. It will have to think about whether they are likely to elicit people's response and thus succeed in achieving their goals.

It is worth examining Indonesian development jargon as it illustrates some underlying attitudes. The interaction between the government and the recipient is usually referred to as "drop", a term which has been absorbed into the Indonesian language. This has the connotation of a gift from above, which is out of your control and perhaps may hit you on the head! Another semantic problem is revealed by the concern over the name used for NGOs. While Non-Government Organization is the term commonly used in the UN, and does not necessarily have any connotations of "anti-government", Indonesian political sensitivities are such that the direct translation of this term "Organisasi Non-Pemerintah" (ORNOP) arouses political concern. For this reason, those who value the contribution that NGOs can make have suggested calling them LPSM (Lembaga Pengembangan Swadaya Masyarakat, that is "People's Self-Reliance Development Groups"). LPSM conveys the idea that these are people's organizations that are also involved in development and are in no way a threat to stability.

One result of the realization by some people in government that NGO activities are relevant and valuable has been the incorporation of some pioneering efforts by NGOs into government programmes. This has happened for some time, with or without acknowledgement. (Examples are the experiences of YAKKUM and YIS in Primary Health Care which have been absorbed into the Ministry of Health's programmes, and the work of the Indonesian Family Planning Association which has been absorbed into BKKBN.) Another result has been overtures from the more open and sympathetic government departments (often urged by the international advisers working with them) to

Indonesian NGOs to become sub-contractors, or to play some role in government projects. On the face of it this seems a desirable marriage. The government can use some of the innovative, pioneering ideas of the NGOs, incorporate them and give them wider coverage. Hopefully, each side can rub off some of its weaknesses and gain some strengths. NGOs often suffer from being too marginal, too hand-to-mouth, too *ad hoc*, and they suffer from political harassment and government suspicion. Being joined to a government project would seem to be a worthwhile step. The government suffers from being too hierarchical and rigid, and excessively top-down. Contact with the NGOs could make them more flexible. In theory each could benefit from the other but experience suggests that this is not always the case.

Similar projects: different methods

When NGOs join government programmes, their collaboration soon shows up structural problems which prevent the theoretical benefits being realized. For us to understand why this collaboration is more difficult than we might expect, we need to look at how the two sides approach similar projects and the very different methods that they employ.

Example 1: Rehabilitation of the Handicapped

Government programme: A national programme of rehabilitation for the handicapped has been carried out by the Department of Social Affairs (with technical assistance and funds from ILO). It consists mainly of training field-workers, providing buildings (called Loka Bina Karya) in a certain number of *kecamatan* capitals, and employing a trained rehabilitation worker to run each one. The LBK is nearly always equipped with a sewing machine and sometimes with other equipment as well. Disabled people may come to the LBK to use the premises and learn skills during the usual working hours. The handicapped person has to reach the LBK him/herself and the programme does not give any other assistance such as loans with which to start a small business.

NGO programme: YPAC–CCPI, an organization based in Solo, has a rural rehabilitation programme for the handicapped (including medical intervention where necessary) in a limited number of specific villages in Central Java. The last stage in the programme is choosing a trade with the handicapped person, providing the training, equipment and capital in his/her own home and helping him/her to run an enterprise. No buildings are provided by foreign NGOs.

Example 2: Village Water Supply

Government programme: A large number of clean water projects are carried out nationally by the Ministry of Health. The ministry receives technical assistance from WHO and UNICEF. Decisions are made at the provincial level as to the technology (piping, pumping, tanks, etc.), the places that will receive it, and the contracts given for its installation. Contractors, who are paid by the units of work completed, often bring in their own workforce from outside and have relatively little contact with villagers who are not trained to maintain and repair the technology.

NGO programme: Yayasan Dian Desa of Yogya have installed a large number of water projects (mostly in Java, Yogyakarta and East Nusatenggara) at the request of villagers. They are only prepared to work in a village if the villagers undertake to help by collecting stones, digging and filling ditches, and carrying pipes. They train a crew from the village in repair and maintenance and are available for consultation in the future if there are problems. Funds come from foreign NGOs.

Example 3: Co-operatives

Government programme: The Co-operatives Service is responsible for setting up KUDs (Village Unit Co-operatives) which, in spite of their name, are situated in *kecamatan* capitals. Their main function is to provide agriculture and fishery inputs at a cheap price and to buy back the produce at an established floor price. They are also able to make loans for agricultural inputs. Their members are land-owners or boat-owners and their officers are appointed, not elected. Technical assistance comes from ILO, Britain and Switzerland.

NGO programme: Bina Swadaya have a programme which has set up Usaha Bersamas (UBs) all over Java and Lampung. These are self-selected credit and loan organizations. After saving for a specified period, the small groups situated in villages can borrow money to start a small business for which all members of the UB are responsible. The UBs choose their own officers. Help for Bina Swadaya comes from foreign NGOs.

Example 4: Banking

Government programme: In theory, Bank Rakyat Indonesia (Bank of the Indonesian People) has three kinds of loans (KIK, KMKP and Mini Kredit) available to the small borrower. Their terms are as low as can be expected. The banks are in *kecamatan* capitals, paperwork is quite complicated and, in spite of the fact that loans are guaranteed by Bank Indonesia and that, in some cases, goods bought with the loan can be their own collateral (*kredit kelayakan*), loan guarantees, usually in the form of land certificates, are nearly always demanded. BKK (Bank Kredit Kecamatan) is more suitable for the rural poor but paying back has to be done once a week in the *kecamatan* capital. The cost of time and transport this entails discourage would-be village clients.

NGO programme: B3K runs a large number of credit unions whose members are able to borrow money with the intention of starting small businesses after they have saved together. These groups arrange their affairs at times and places to suit themselves and the members of the group guarantee each other's loans against default.

It is unlikely that the government officials responsible for the government programmes know about the parallel NGO programmes, at least at the provincial level and below. If they have heard of any such schemes they are likely to be suspicious of them. NGOs, on the other hand, are frequently cynical and sceptical of the value of government programmes. We need to examine the reasons for these tensions more closely.

Tension

Many officials at the provincial level and below, see NGOs as amateurs and meddlers in the business of development. Such people consider that they have received special training and have special responsibilities in their field. In the course of the promotion of complete loyalty to GOLKAR and PANCASILA alone, government officials are encouraged to think of the government as the sole agent of development, and of all other agents as unimportant and peripheral. While government officials generally agree that NGOs have a role to play in welfare (hospitals, orphanages and the handicapped) and indeed have started government-sponsored NGOs to help them (Yayasan Dharmais), they generally consider that NGO efforts outside the field of welfare are likely to:

(i) encourage a split between the people and the government;

(ii) encourage religious extremism and disunity;

(iii) confuse the people about the aims of the government and destabilize the people;

(iv) expose government mistakes and shortcomings and cause government officials to lose face; *and*

(v) be of no significance at the national level since all important decisions are made by the government.

On the other hand, NGOs think of government programmes as limited by the structures they have to work through, above all the civil service. While they are prepared to grant that the government often means well, they suggest that government programmes cannot conscientiously and efficiently reach the rural poor in ways that will help them if they are implemented through government machinery. From the NGO point of view, the most noticeable characteristic of a civil servant is that they are interested less in the actual benefits to the rural poor and more in personal aggrandizement. They would see the bureaucracy in the same way as Glassburner:

Petty corruption is rife in the bureaucracy, primarily because the scale of government salaries is so poor that officials are forced either to moonlight, at least partly, on government time, or to charge extra-ordinary fees for services rendered to users of government services, or both.[9]

Civil servants are thought of as playing elaborate games whereby unrealistic instructions are received from the top, are subverted or misapplied, and glowing reports of success are sent back up the line. Some NGOs believe that high officials are well aware of how corrupt their subordinates are and knowingly participate in the charade as a way of helping their subordinates to supplement their income. Generally programmes are thought likely to:

    (i) benefit only civil servants and the village élites;
   (ii) have their funds subverted by civil servants;
  (iii) put monopolistic control over development activities into the hands of civil servants and village élites;
  (iv) be badly targeted because they are usually based on bad research; *and*
   (v) be based on an unclear understanding of the local situation because centralized planning is based on civil servants reporting problems up the chain of command with scant regard to reality.

Not surprisingly there is suspicion and distrust between the two groups. This can often be reconciled at the national level, but it is still very strong at the provincial level and below. Thus, although the leaders of NGOs and government departments can agree on aims and ways of working, this agreement is often missing at the lower levels. Any government programmes that wish to encourage local decision-making, participation, flexibility, bottom-up planning and accountability (all of which are areas in which NGOs have particular strength), will run into considerable difficulties with their own officials whose existence is based on transmitting instructions from above, giving orders to people below them, strictly obeying instructions received (or making a show of it), and keeping the boss happy. Also not surprisingly, NGOs which have been subcontracted to help implement such programmes or train others to do so, find passive or active opposition at the lower levels.

Collaboration?

Why, it may be asked, should NGOs want to work with the government if their understanding is so cynical? The answers could be among the following:

    (i) After such a long time out in the cold, they are happy to receive public recognition of their work.

(ii) The government has money (its own or borrowed) to spend and NGOs are usually hard up. They want a slice of the cake.

(iii) NGOs like to have the opportunity to play on the big table (i.e., to be part of large, even nationwide, development programmes).

(iv) NGOs still nurture a belief that they can effect a change in the way that the government works.

With some knowledge of the conceptions and misconceptions which the government and NGOs have of each other, and their structural dissimilarities, it is instructive to look at a few examples where NGOs and government have tried to work together.

Example 1

An agreement was drawn up between an NGO, the local government and a funding agency by which the NGO would install a clean-water supply for three villages on the slopes of a mountain, and the government would be responsible for the further maintenance of the project and for the development of village industries which could be founded on the surplus of water available.

After the drinking-water system was installed, however, the government replaced all the people who had been trained in maintenance techniques by the NGO, and only helped those villagers who had the capital to utilize the new water (e.g., with clove seedlings or fish ponds). The project was considered a success by the government who asked for it to be replicated in other areas. When the funding agency pointed out that the village rich had got richer from the ancillary benefits but the poor had not, there was a problem in defining the difference between *village* development and *villagers'* development, and a secondary structural problem as the only government programmes that could assist with capital formation to take advantage of the water were bank loans which were unobtainable by the poor who had no collateral.

Example 2

An agreement was drawn up between an NGO, BKKBN and a funding agency whereby money was to be made available to groups of people accepting contraception from BKKBN, as an incentive for them to start small enterprises. The necessary training in capital formation and money management for these groups was to be done by the NGO because it was considered that they had lengthy experience in this field. On being introduced to the groups of contraceptive accepters, the NGO realized that these were groups linked only by the fact that they received contraceptive devices from BKKBN. It was therefore necessary to begin with group-formation training so that the necessary solidarity could be achieved. The NGO soon discovered that BKKBN's chief objective was to distribute the money that they had received from the donor agency quickly, and that they were unable to accept the time span needed to prepare the groups to receive the money so that it could be usefully applied (even though this was the recognized skill for which the NGO had been hired).

Example 3

An NGO was requested to train villagers in bottom-up development strategy. The understanding was that the government agencies would follow up and give guidance on the plans that the villagers drew up. When valid plans were drawn up by villagers, *kecamatan*-level government officials did nothing to help them and thus the impetus and self-confidence of the villagers decreased.

Example 4

An NGO was requested by the government to train civil servants in improved stove technology. Care was taken by the NGO to emphasize that skills were needed to make the stoves and each had to be made to fit in with existing patterns of cooking and stove use, which needed to be investigated first. Shortly afterwards, an order was issued that stoves of a particular design were to be built everywhere. In many cases they worked less well than the existing stoves, and the idea of fuel-efficient stoves was discredited in the minds of the villagers.

These cautionary tales illustrate the dangers inherent in mixing NGO and government styles of work. It seems likely that the government will become increasingly cognizant of NGO activities, and that there will be increasing attempts to incorporate them or their ideas into government programmes. There are good possibilities for the cross fertilization of ideas but attention must be paid to the interface between the idea and the structure available to implement the idea. This has not previously happened to any great extent. It was assumed that good NGO ideas and practice could be turned into good government ideas and practice simply by order.

The quality of human-development programmes is very much dictated by the structure through which these programmes are implemented. NGO projects are nearly always based on particular circumstances, whereas governments nearly always look at the broad canvas. As Emmerson remarks, "Government can pick up a successful pilot project and rapidly inflate it to national proportions, ignoring the role of particular circumstances in the original circumstances."[10]

The strengths of NGOs lie in their appreciation of the particular; many of their initiatives can be deformed and spoilt if they are accepted and disseminated too fast.[11] The government, which has the job of implementing development in 27 provinces, sometimes finds the need for slow progress irksome and wants to start big programmes. The basic dilemma is that while NGOs can put a lot of effort and time into small projects and make them work, these cannot necessarily be transformed into the needs of government bodies which think in terms of provinces, if not the whole of Indonesia. There is room for collaboration and there is room for pioneer work by NGOs to be absorbed without killing it. Such collaboration, however, is difficult and requires an openness and give-and-take which is not always present.

NOTES
1. The World Bank's *World Development Report* 1983 (World Bank: Washington, DC) gives most of these facts. Comparison countries used to be India, Pakistan and Bangladesh, but now quoted are the Philippines, Malaysia, Turkey, Brazil.
2. See *Financial Constraints and Human Development in the Eighties* (World Bank: Washington, DC, 1983), pp. 104–161.
3. Many such stories have been carried by Indonesian newspapers in July 1983.
4. World Bank, ibid., and PPSK-UGM, (the Centre for Village and Regional Studies at Gadja Mada University: Jogjakarta, Indonesia), July 1983.
5. "Human development" is used here according to the World Bank definition: "population, labor, employment, education, health, nutrition, housing, water supply and sanitation."
6. Karl Jackson, "The political implications of structure and culture in Indonesia" in K. Jackson and L. Pye (eds), *Political Power and Communications in Indonesia* (University of California Press: Berkeley, Los Angeles, 1978).
7. Donald Emmerson, "The Bureaucracy in Political Context – Weakness in Strength" in Jackson and Pye (eds), op. cit.
8. The *arisan* is a women's social gathering at which money is collected from the participants and distributed according to need, or by lottery, to each person in turn.
9. Bruce Glassburner, "Indonesia's new economic policy and its sociopolitical implications" in Jackson and Pye, op. cit.
10. D. Emmerson, op. cit.
11. See Glen Williams, "Community participation and voluntary agencies in Indonesia" in *Prisma* ("The Indonesian Indicator"), no. 16, March 1980.

11. Strengthening Community-Based Technology Management Systems[1]

by James Terrent and Hasan Poerbo

This chapter describes the work of two organizations that have been concerned with alternatives to the Indonesian Government's structure for village administration, as it relates to rural development at the village level. The first organization, the Centre for Environmental Studies at the University of Technology, Bandung (CES–ITB), started the work that centred around the village of Ciamis, and it was subsequently carried on by the Institute of Development Studies (LSP). Hasan Poerbo is the Head of the CES–ITB, and James Terrent was a graduate student working with him.

In Indonesia, as in many other countries, erosion and flood-control problems in river basins with high population densities have become widespread phenomena and a national concern. In part, the problem is rooted in the poverty and farming practices of the people who live in these river basins. Attempts at corrective action by the government have had only marginal effects. Highly centralized in their management and heavily subsidized, these government schemes become bogged down in their own rigidity and are too costly for replication on a large scale.

In 1980, the CES–ITB undertook a Participatory Action Research (PAR) programme in the uplands of the Citanduy River Basin in the "Regency" (or *kabupaten*) of Ciamis in West Java, Indonesia. Through an action-learning process,

The Government as the Definer of "Development"

*"He complains there is acute poverty and
unemployment here! Remind me to order more banks
for giving loans to be opened in this area!"*

Source: Cartoon by R.K. Laxman in *New Internationalist*, April 1981; first
published in *The Times of India*.

this programme sought to develop experience with a
different approach in which people mobilize their own
resources to address the problem, with the government
assuming the role of enabler and service provider.

The setting

Of the total 446,000 hectares that comprise the Citanduy

River Basin, 27 per cent are classified as uplands devoted to small-farmer cultivation. The population density of 654 persons per square kilometre is quite high by world standards, especially for uplands areas. The average size of agricultural-land holding is 0.5 hectares per household. There is also a sizeable landless population.[2]

Thirteen per cent of the land area in the basin is classified as "critical land", which means that it is too degraded to sustain a permanent staple agricultural crop, though in fact some of these lands are still cultivated – providing at best only a marginal return. Fortunately, the condition of these lands is usually reversible through proper soil and water management practices.

The Indonesian government has been aware of the need for improved watershed management for some time, leading in 1980 to the USAID-funded Citanduy II Project, which sought to develop the capacity of local and regional governments collaborating with the Ministry of Agriculture to implement a programme of watershed improvement. This programme provided substantial subsidies to groups of farmers in order to motivate them to establish 10-hectare terraced demonstration plots on which an approved uplands-farming system technology package was applied. Working out of the demonstration plots, extension agents encouraged farmers in an expansion area around the site to adopt the same practices, offering them somewhat smaller subsidies as an incentive.

At roughly the same time as Citanduy II was being initiated, the newly formed CES–ITB was asked by the Ministry of Population and Environment to undertake a policy review of the government's upland-development effort. The Centre's study concluded that existing government programmes suffered from the fact that programmes were being planned and implemented without an adequate knowledge of traditional attitudes and farming practices. These programmes also used inappropriate approaches and incentives in their attempts to induce farmers to change their existing practices, with the result that they often reverted back to their old practices as soon as the subsidies were no longer available. Members of the centre felt that the best way to substantiate their findings would be to demonstrate the validity of an alternative approach.

The experimental programme

The experimental programme was initiated on two sites in late 1980: Sagalaherang Village, with a population of some 4,000, and Cigaru Hamlet, with a population of about 700.[3] Both sites were characterized by the substantial independence of individual households in decision-making and income-generating activities. Participation in joint decision making and co-operative activities was limited at both hamlet and village levels.[4]

Cigaru, though socially relatively more homogeneous, was much the poorer of the two sites. A sizeable portion of its male labour force spent substantial time away from the community in search of income-earning opportunities. This gave them less time for activities such as terracing and irrigation development in order to improve the productivity of their lands. Available data indicated that crop yields were declining in the late 1970s and early 1980, especially in Cigaru.

Sagalaherang was more socially stratified. A relatively small number of large land-owners had become heavily involved in cash crops, especially tree-crop agriculture; a larger number of middle-level farmers marketed some surpluses from their production; while the largest group of households consisted of small subsistence farmers. The first two groups dominated village decision-making, especially on economic matters. The third group had little access to this process.

Preparatory activities

The first year of the programme was devoted to the collection of baseline data and the formation of a programme strategy, followed by initial field motivation and organizing efforts. A variety of techniques were used to engage the villagers in a critical assessment of their reality and of the measures they might take to improve their situation. These included brainstorming, directed discussion of specific community problems, simple simulations, and the reading and discussion of passages from the Quran. Considerable attention was given to "critical introspection" aimed at identifying the major attitudinal and organizational barriers confronting community-wide development. Villagers were helped to look at problems logically and to examine their systematic causes. This was intended to be a process of self-education and changing attitudes, as well as a stimulus to organized action.

As the programme progressed, staff came to recognize that women were active members of the agricultural labour force in both settings. Though they played only a minor role in public functions, in the household they were equal partners with their husbands in decision making. Consequently, attention was given to involving them more actively in the discussions and simulations. This led to a number of women's activities centred on the intensification of home gardening, animal husbandry, child and health care, housing improvement, etc.

Reactions to the programme were significantly different in Sagalaherang and Cigaru. In Sagalaherang, the point of entry had been through the village head and his assistants. It was a new village, recently created through the division of another village that had grown too large for efficient village administration. Here, the village head insisted that the CES–ITB work with and through the formal village government rather than calling a mass meeting for discussion and informal education, as was done in Cigaru. Yet the village head and the official governing council of the village made little effort to inform or involve other village residents in the initial motivation, planning and organization. This seriously weakened the programme from the start, a problem that was never overcome and is reflected in the limited results achieved there.

By contrast, the hamlet chief in Cigaru was open-minded and himself a small farmer. He was also the village dresser, informal veterinarian, and birth attendant[5] who was genuinely respected and regularly consulted for guidance by the villagers. He facilitated the broad participation of the hamlet residents in the programme and was active in the formation of the subsequent work groups. Consequently, it was possible in Cigaru to develop a broad organizational base from which a strong, community-based development programme emerged.

Developing an action programme

In May 1981, residents of both communities were asked to come up with a list of priorities for an action programme. In Cigaru, they listed: improved roads, a market, electricity and drinking-water supplies, and improved seeds and agricultural inputs. In Sagalaherang they listed: the improvement of the village council, better seeds and agricultural inputs, electricity, and improved village-market facilities.

Cigaru's choice of activities such as roads and a market assumed a significant marketable agriculture surplus that did not yet exist in the village. Also electricity would require a level of income and management capability far beyond their actual situation. The need for improvements in land and water management as a basis for other economic development efforts was not mentioned. These issues were explored with the residents in mass meetings.

Project staff then invited the residents to visit a nearby experimental project site at Panawangan that demonstrated terracing- and cropping-system improvements. The result was a decision to start with a simple programme of bench terracing and improvements in water distribution and drainage, along with experimentation with dry-season planting of various legumes and other vegetables.

In both communities, bench terracing and integrated-farming techniques were demonstrated on a plot of 0.5 hectare – the size of the typical small farm plot – donated by the communities. Working voluntarily on the demonstration plot, farmers learned the terracing techniques, which were later applied to their own lands.

To carry out the arduous terracing of their own fields, the Cigaru farmers formed themselves into *kelompok hamparan* ("coverage groups"). Generally, such a group was comprised of farmers who tilled adjoining plots in single mini-watershed areas. Their activities were initially co-ordinated through meetings of the *rembug desa*, the traditional mass meetings held to co-ordinate village matters. The CES–ITB team usually joined in these events. Similar groups were formed in Sagalaherang, but it became evident that the programme was being implemented mainly by the larger élite farmers (who dominated village decision making), on their own land, and through the use of hired labourers to do the terracing – without explaining its purpose. Only a relatively small area was improved. The CES–ITB field team eventually decided to abandon their activities in Sagalaherang.

The further evolution of village structures in Cigaru

With time and experience, the effort in Cigaru continued to evolve, and farmers experimented with different organizational structures as they became aware of the need for the internal co-ordination of their efforts. As household agricultural plots tended to be both small and widely scattered, due to inheritance patterns and new purchases of land, some farmers found that they belonged to more than one *kelompok hamparan*. This resulted in an uneven distribution of obligations for labour sharing.

This problem led them to form what they called *kelompok domisili* (domicile groups) based on neighbourhood blocks of approximately 25 to 35 households each. The total area of terraced farmland increased by 41 per cent over that which was originally planned as a result of the improved division of labour. The *kelompok domisili* became the locus for further efforts to improve local-resource management and integrate new technologies into community and household production systems. These groups also undertook a wide variety of new initiatives including housing rehabilitation; the resettlement of homes on steep, erosion-prone slopes; animal husbandry; the intensification of home gardens, home-processing and cottage industries; co-operative child care; and the introduction of energy-saving stoves, etc. They became particularly important in the village communication process, serving as communication nodes for the discussion of community issues, and the sharing of ideas and technologies.

During the first year, CES–ITB also encouraged the development of functional groups, (e.g., dry-land farmers' groups, irrigation-user groups, sheep-pen groups, etc). The domicile groups linked the various functional groups to communities and became part of the social fabric of the village.

At one point, the community needed to acquire a sprayer to combat a blight through the application of pesticides. The CES–ITB field team used the opportunity to call a meeting between the dry-land farmer groups, to buy a sprayer that would be shared among them. This led to the establishment of the *kelompok usaha bersama ekonomi*

(KUBE), a hamlet-level co-operative organization. Once formed, this group assumed a growing range of functions that strengthened the base-level organizations and helped link them into the larger governmental and market structures, while protecting members from being exploited by other political and economic power-holders including the official village council, larger commercial farmers, traders, and money-lenders. Specific functions of the KUBE included the following:

(i) Providing a forum within which members co-ordinated their cropping systems to facilitate the collective purchase and distribution of agricultural inputs such as seeds, fertilizers and insecticides, as well as the co-operative marketing of their increased agricultural produce.

(ii) Providing a management body for pre- and post-agricultural processing and support activities such as compost making, animal husbandry, seed nurseries, and processing and storage facilities.

(iii) Operating a savings and loan association for the community, thus generating relatively small amounts of capital for individual needs such as home construction and improvement, and agricultural inputs, as well as for community undertakings.

Legally, co-operatives can only exist at village level and above in Indonesia, in the form of the government-sponsored KUD (Village Unit Co-operative). This arrangement has several limitations. First, as a village-level organization, it is often geographically distant from individual hamlets so that the frequency of its use is limited. Moreover, formal membership of the KUD is frequently limited to farmers with relatively large land holdings, or those participating in a government agricultural programme and more specifically the government's rice-production programme. KUD participation by farmers with half a hectare or less is rare. Second, its function is limited largely to distributing inputs and marketing crops, thus preventing it from becoming a more integral part of the wider village economy. Third, as a government-sponsored institution, it is governed by the village élite acting partly on the basis of directives coming from district and subdistrict levels of government. And, as is true in much of Asia, there is a widespread distrust of government-sponsored co-operatives because of a past history of mismanagement.

In all these respects, the structure and the function of the KUD generally reflect the wider problem of limited participation by the weaker members of the community, especially those in upland, rural settlements. The KUBE provided the basis for an alternative structure that may ultimately transform and strengthen the KUD. It is an intermediate co-operative organization which itself is a direct outgrowth of the activities of smaller functional organizations and domicile groups. Thus, it is strongly based in activities specifically geared to the interests of, and controlled by, the formerly weak members of the community. By this time the whole hamlet had become structurally transformed, becoming a kind of a "development module" available for replication by other hamlets.

Expansion to other hamlets

The programme gained considerable visibility and stature within the area as a result of a visit to Cigaru from the Minister of State for the Environment in August 1981. Responding to the interest expressed by surrounding communities, the CES–ITB field team encouraged some Cigaru farmers to teach visitors from other hamlets what they had learned. They called on the Quranic injunction that a wise and good man shares his knowledge rather than use it only for private gain. Soon, meetings were being organized in the farmers' fields, attended by as many as 200 people at a time.

The villages represented at these meetings were at different levels of economic development, resource endowment, and institutional strength. Some were lowland villages where the major economic activity was the production of irrigated rice. Each brought back ideas suited for adaptation to their specific needs. Some formed irrigaters' associations. Others started with land consolidation and reapportioning.

Usually attention was given to the development of organizations that approximated the Cigaru structure. Indeed, in some of the villages near Cigaru, the farmers organized themselves more quickly and with a higher level of participation, both in numbers and degree of involvement, than had occurred during the corresponding period in Cigaru the year before. In part, this was a result of their being able to take note of what had and had not worked in Cigaru. At the same time, it must be recognized that Cigaru had been one of the least developed villages in the region and was burdened by a steady flight of its working-age population, as well as by a weak and remote relationship with the district-level government.

By mid 1983, participation in what was now being called the "Cigaru Model" had spread to at least 24 hamlets of 14 villages in Ciamis district. Some 3,000 hectares had been terraced without direct subsidies.[6] The cases of Sukadana and Karangpari villages illustrate two different models of how the Cigaru Model is disseminated.

Sukadana is representative of "second-generation villages" in which the CES–ITB took the initiative in inviting village leaders to visit Cigaru, and later assisted them in implementing the programme in their own villages, with some of the best group leaders from Cigaru acting as "instructors". Generally, the CES–ITB team was called in only when there was a question that the farmer-"instructors" from Cigaru were not able to explain, and Sukadana's leaders came to the team asking for advice. Thus, the CES–ITB presence was much lower than it had been in Cigaru itself.

Karangpari represented a "third-generation village" in which the transfer was entirely spontaneous. The leader of a sub-hamlet in Karangpari heard about Cigaru's experience and went to have a look. He came back from Cigaru convinced that this sub-hamlet could replicate, and perhaps even improve on, what Cigaru had accomplished. He invited all of the households in the sub-hamlet to organize a "picnic" in Cigaru and have a discussion with the Cigaru community. Within three months, his sub-hamlet had implemented all they had learned and more, in turn becoming a model for the other sub-hamlets in Karangpari. Within a year, the entire village had adopted the Cigaru model, with minimal assistance from CES–ITB.

In addition to the 24 hamlets specifically identified earlier by CES–ITB as having adopted the Cigaru model, there were others which built on the experience of the second- and third-generation villages which the CES–ITB did not monitor. From early 1986 onwards, CES–ITB estimated that the model had been adopted by some 40 to 50 hamlets in 26 villages.

Creating an area-oriented development foundation

By mid 1982, the Ciamis Programme had become so complex and had been extended to so many villages that CES–ITB could no longer adequately respond to the growth in technical and training needs at the level of attention that was required. It was evident that the participating villages would need to draw on government sources for more of their needs. In some instances this was already occurring, but in others there was need for a brokering role to help both parties learn to work together productively. There was need for an intermediary organization that would perform such a brokering role between the hamlet-level organizations and the public- and private-sector organizations with which they needed to establish and manage relationships.

To perform this function it was proposed that a non-profit making, area-oriented development foundation should be established. Among its tasks would be:

(i) To act as broker/consultant to KUBEs in their negotiation with government rural banks to obtain larger agricultural and economic development loans, using a trust fund developed from the KUBE's savings and loan association as collateral.

(ii) To serve as a clearing house for technical assistance in addressing environmental and agro-economic problems peculiar to the upland areas of the Citanduy River Basin.

(iii) To provide training for community cadres (village farmers, women and youths) to support the practical application of integrated rural/environmental development techniques within their own communities, and to serve as trainers/disseminators for other communities.

(iv) To up-grade extension officers from the agricultural and other ministries and to train them in the motivational and organizational techniques involved in the Cigaru model.

(v) To monitor and evaluate progress toward integrated rural/environmental development in Ciamis district and to identify key constraints.

In 1985, with the encouragement of the Ciamis district head, who had been a constant supporter of the Ciamis Programme, the Yayasan Bina Lingkungan Hidup (YBLH, Foundation for the Advancement of the Environment) was established in the Ciamis township. The CES–ITB field team formed the core staff of the new foundation. Financed by a small grant from CUSO, the *Lembaga Studi Pembangunan* (LSP, the Institute for Development Studies), a national NGO, assumed many of the technical support functions previously provided for the team by the CES–ITB. The chairperson of the YBLH also served as chair person of a local Co-operative High School Foundation (SMAK), which intended to train young people from the villages for managerial responsibilities in the KUBEs after their graduation.

Lessons and future directions

The foundation of the success of the Ciamis programme was established by inducing one hamlet, Cigaru, to come to grips with the need to improve the management of its land and water-resource base, by creating grassroots organizational structures compatible with the traditions and skills of its people, and by gradually building up their capacity to confront more and more complex problems. It was perhaps fortunate that this occurred in one of the most undeveloped communities in the immediate area. This made Cigaru's success all the more impressive for the surrounding communities and left them confident that if Cigaru could do it, so could they – perhaps even better.

From there, the dissemination was lateral – from hamlet to hamlet and farmer to farmer. Programme personnel mainly facilitated this process, allowing farmers to share the hard-won lessons of their own experimentation, in addition to what they had learned from the "experts".

Villagers learned about the potentials of what could be accomplished through the application of their own social energy and through the improved management of locally available resources. They also learned the values of co-operative action. They were strengthening their own technology-management systems, by which they captured new ideas from a variety of sources, tested and adapted them to varied local conditions, and then shared them with one another.

Once sufficient KUBEs have been formed, the intention is to unite them in an association that can operate as a KUBE-owned, non-bank institution linking them into the larger resource networks of the national banking system. Eventually this association may be integrated into the KUD system, thereby gaining a legitimacy that will facilitate access to other government programmes while the control over resources is retained by the KUBEs.

The Ciamis Programme experience demonstrates that a transformation of the traditional village social fabric is possible through a bottom-up social learning process that mobilizes the social energy of the people as a critical development resource. And it makes a small contribution towards a better understanding of how this may be accomplished on a broader scale through a combination of public and private initiative. But the challenge of achieving effective vertical integration into the larger social, economic, and political structures remains. There is a long road yet to be travelled in obtaining a general acceptance of such an approach by national-policy makers and adapting it for implementation on a larger scale.

Notes
1. This article first appeared in David C. Korten (ed.), *Community Management, Asian Experience and Perspectives* (Kumarian Press: West Hartford, Connecticut, 1986), pp. 172–182.

2. USAID Indonesia, Citanduy II Project Paper (USAID: Washington, DC, August 1980).
3. The *kampung*, or hamlet, is the smallest formal settlement unit in Java.
4. Judistira Carna and Ade Emka (eds), "Studi Pengetahuan, Sikap dan Praktek Masyarakat Kampung Cigaru Dalam Program Lingkungan Pedesaan Terpadu", a report published by PSLH–ITB (the Environmental Studies Centre at the Institute of Technology): Bandung, 1983.
5. This is a very unusual position for a male in Sunda culture.
6. Apart from small initial amounts of capital, seeds, fertilizers, pesticides and equipment (which farmers repaid directly to the programme or by revolving contributions to other communities), the only subsidy of the Ciamis Programme was in the time of the programme staff.

12. Encouraging the Poor to Help Themselves

by M. Zainuddin and Patrick Sweeting

This chapter consists of two parts: M. Zainuddin's description of LP3ES work in Klaten, Central Java, in economic development and community organizing; and a commentary on it by Patrick Sweeting of OXFAM, Indonesia.

Zainuddin's piece describes the work of the Indonesian NGO LP3ES (whose Indonesian acronym translates as the Institute for Socio-Economic Research, Education, and Information). Since 1982, their Klaten field office has been engaged in a process of helping the very poor to improve their own incomes and escape from depending on charity. It has strongly emphasized personal motivation and brought Islam and its values into the process of rural development. The piece was written for the 1988 ILO (International Labour Organisation) Regional Trainers' Workshop in Participatory Rural Development, organized by ILO, CUSO and FNS (Friedrich Neuman Stiftung), and held in Tagtaytay in the Philippines. Patrick Sweeting's commentary comes from development education materials put out by OXFAM on the work of LP3ES.

Encouraging the Poor to Help Themselves

by M. Zainuddin

In 1982 I felt the need (and saw the opportunity) to use the traditional Islamic charitable tax system of *zakat* as a means of helping the poorest rural people to escape from poverty. *Zakat* is the annual yearly hand-out from the local mosque

"Leakages" and the Resultant Weakening of Government Policies

"You might just as well stay there – there's just not enough water to go round."

Source: Cartoon by Richard Wilson, reproduced by kind permission of *Development Forum*, a magazine published by the UN Division for Economic and Social Information, and the United Nations University: New York.

of food and clothing for the poorest members of the community. It is raised from a tax levied on those who worship at the mosque and are considered to have the ability to pay. This donation occurs only once a year and its long-term result is that the same people are around the next year, still very poor. I made contact with the local branch of Mohammediyah (a national Indonesian Islamic reformist organization) who agreed that in 1982 the 180,000 Indonesian Rupiah (Rps) that they had collected for *zakat* alms could be channelled through a different system – one of community organization and community development.

Sixteen *mustahiq* (those who are the poorest in the community and who thus have the right to receive the *zakat*) were approached and, after long discussions, agreed that they would form a group and would not immediately consume their share of the *zakat*, but would save the money together as a fund for income-generation and productive enterprises, and would help their own members to escape from their poverty. For two years this group met at my house every fortnight, discussed their situation, reinforced their collective determination to escape from poverty, and started to use the *zakat* funds to start up small-business enterprises. Savings from these activities were put back into the common pool.

At the end of two years, the lives of the original 16 had changed in the following ways: four people had changed from being *mustahiq* to being well enough off to be taxed in turn to give *zakad* (*muzakhi*); two people who were previously unemployed became small traders; three people who were already self-employed in a very small way increased their business by 125 per cent; four people who previously had nothing but their labour to sell bought their own sewing machines and set themselves up in business; and three remained poor and their lives had few changes.

Based on these results, I set up a project called "The Household Economy" with the expressed intention of getting away from a relief and charitable approach to the rural poor, and towards an approach which emphasized encouraging them to become self-sufficient. Klaten, the area in which the project took place, is the third most populated, but the second smallest district of Central Java. Just over half of the cultivated land is under irrigated-rice farming and encroachments are steadily being made on this land for housing, offices and roads. The population is growing and 50 per cent are landless.

One basic principle in this programme was, and is, that the target group of the rural poor are involved as much as possible at every stage of the activity, from planning through implementation and monitoring, to evaluation. The project is not something done to the poor, but something the poor, with the help of a few sensitive facilitators, do for themselves. Another principle is that problems are solved in an integrated way – all aspects of a problem are looked at and approaches to solving the problem are considered together. A third principle is to try and identify and develop local potential, local resources, and local leadership. The methodology is as in the figure on the page opposite.

The first and most important activity is to raise awareness amongst the poor that their fate can be changed by their own strength. Discussions involve reflections on Islam, on Javanese traditions and mythology, and on their present state, as well as comparisons with other systems. Once a level of awareness about future possibilities is reached, it becomes necessary (and possible) to increase people's knowledge and productive skills. People are encouraged to form themselves into groups which are called UBs, that is *Usaha Bersama* ("joint efforts"). The group works out what kind of training it needs, and LP3ES attempts to provide this. The training is usually based on the need for managing the group, basic entrepreneurship, and productive skills.

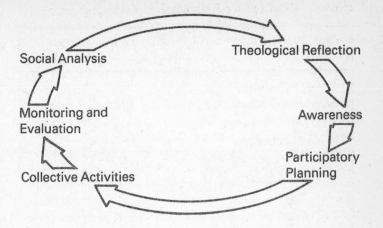

The only way out of poverty is for the people to form small co-operatives, and gradually to build up into one larger co-operative. Once the small co-operatives have been solidly formed – and have a discipline of saving, investment and repayment – then they can be helped by judicious soft loans from outside. It is important that the groups depend upon their own resources at first, but it is also true that they will only be able to amass very small amounts of capital from their own resources. Once group consciousness and financial discipline have been learnt, then infusions of funds from outside can speed up the rate at which they can turn over the money, pay back their loans, and increase their own incomes. Between 1984 and 1987, 104 productive groups were formed. New enterprises were started, existing micro-enterprises expanded, and jobs created, as can be seen from the following table on p. 182.

The experiences of working together has convinced these people of the benefits of a group, and the value of

Growth of Productive Activities

Type of Productive	Total of the Groups			
Activities	1984	1985	1986	1987
1. Garden cultivation	11	14	8	22
2. Roadside stalls	16	10	13	17
3. Poultry breeding	6	6	5	15
4. Cattle breeding	6	6	25	34
5. Fresh water fishery	1	14	13	15
6. Home industry food processing	–	–	3	6
7. Services	–	–	3	12
8. Beekeeping	–	–	–	1
TOTAL	40	50	70	122

savings. One of the clear benefits is that they are no longer dependent upon securing loans from money-lenders at very high rates of interest – their own group becomes the money-lender, and they have a say in how the money is lent. In 1984, all groups could only mobilize Rps 11,700,000. By 1987, this has risen to Rps 33.5 million. And all the members of these groups started as *mustahiq* (receivers of *zakat* alms). The criteria for determining who were to be *mustahiq* were that they should be people who earned less than Rps 1,500 a day, had no permanent job, owned less than 0.3 hectares, and whose house was only made of temporary materials.

The next stage is for the 104 groups (representing 1,606 households or about 9,639 people) to co-ordinate their business activities through an Inter-Group Coalition for

Co-operation. In time, this will become an official co-operative – an independent and functional co-operative which has bottom-up planning created from, by, and for its members. A co-operative such as this constitutes a people's movement.

Commentary on LP3ES Klaten

by Patrick Sweeting

So far, the project has been very successful in arousing a feeling of solidarity among the rural community and in showing that a household economy can develop through group effort.

The wider political implications of this poverty-oriented project have not been overlooked. In most villages the officials are relatively wealthy and act as money-lenders. The UB groups will create alternative sources of credit for poorer villagers who will no longer be dependent on the patronage of the village officials, not least because they frequently belong to different political parties. It is hoped that LP3ES, which is a neutral organization, will encourage the motivators to steer clear of village politics. An observer has remarked in a personal communication that

> the political aspects are only an offshoot of a programme which is setting up alternative lines of wealth, but this upsets the whole political/financial patronage that percolates throughout the Indonesian political system. However, we must realize that this is likely to cause some problems in future – in my opinion good problems which we should be aware of and try to control to a limited extent, but which we can really only face as and when they arise.

Further complications came in LP3ES's dealings with the

local government. First, there were difficulties with the Department of Co-operatives. In Indonesia, *Koperasi* (co-operatives) are a product of a government department and it is very difficult for one, however well it is community-based, to be given a certificate from the government if the government has not started the co-operative and allowed it to borrow money from banks. Furthermore, the government will not allow any organization to call itself a co-operative if it is not registered and practising within the government system. Organizations like LP3ES which have co-operatives, have to go through the charade of calling their groups *Pra-Kooperasi* (pre-co-operatives) so that they don't offend the local branches of the Department of Co-operatives. In a tactic which has become quite usual in Indonesia, they find a sympathetic high-level official in Jakarta to give them permission to operate, and use this as their passport with the sub-regional officials who would otherwise block their work.

In the case of the Kridopakitien group, there were mismatches with the Ministry of Agriculture. The extension arms of this ministry had many high-quality fruit-tree seedlings available at a price to farmers who could pay. None of the Kridopakitien group could individually afford to buy into such high-production possibilities. Only as a group were they able to take advantage of the research and development of the local extension workers. If LP3ES had not been successful in helping the people to create their own groups and mobilize their own savings, there is no way that they could have gained access to such valuable inputs.

13. Good Manners with the Rural Poor

by David Watson and Team, and Tatta Issa

This article is a reprint of one part of a training course designed in Indonesia for government planners at the sub-regional level (Local Government Training II – DEPNAGRI (the Indonesian Ministry for the Interior) and USAID). The course was designed to give Indonesian government planners "an opportunity to develop a 'feel' for what it is like to be poor". The materials seek to educate planners in sound research practices and skills as well as to begin to mould the attitudes of trainees. This unit of the course illustrates how inappropriate attitudes on the part of government officials towards the poor preclude their involvement in poverty-programme planning. David Watson, an adult educator and training specialist, was the leader of the team involved in this project. He lived in Indonesia for four years and speaks the language. Tatta Issa was the artist.

Trainer's guide

Objective: to improve participants' approach to rural research involving face-to-face contact with respondents at village level.

Process: there are several alternative ways of using these materials, after introducing the session's objectives:

1. (a) show all the pictures on the overhead projector (OHP) for about 10 seconds each, with no commentary.
   (b) repeat each picture in turn on the OHP and ask: What is happening? What are the most striking features of the scene to you? What conclusions can you draw about the completeness and accuracy of the data these researches will collect?
   (c) ask the trainees to sum up the "do's" and "don't's" at the end.

All the Participants in a Food-for-Work Scheme in Bangladesh

Source: Village teaching materials used by Proshika MUK, a Bangladesh NGO, 1984.

2. (a) Show each picture on the OHP briefly, then repeat pictures 1, 3, 5, 7, 9, 11 and ask the same questions as at 1(b) above, but with the extra question: How would you handle this interview differently?

  (b) make a note of trainees' comments on the board.

  (c) display pictures 2, 4, 6, 8, 10, 12 and ask the trainees to relate their comments to the scenes depicted.

3. (a) Show each picture briefly on the OHP then split the trainees into several work groups, distribute versions of the pictures to each group, and ask the questions as at 1(b) above.

  (b) have a plenary report back from each group and ask for supplementary remarks from the other groups.

1. TRAINER'S NOTE (do not show to trainee)
○ scene is the centre of village (not remote)
○ lack of consideration by driver
○ passengers attracting attention to themselves
○ vehicles in convoy
○ evidence of frivolous, casual approach
○ dress ostentatious (collar/tie)

2. TRAINER'S NOTE
○ researcher's dress modest
○ walking
○ looking on appreciatively
○ not interrupting work activity
○ not making notes
○ pleasant non-threatening behaviour
○ not in centre of village

3. TRAINER'S NOTE
- ○ ostentatious, unsuitable city garb
- ○ jewellery, watch, cigarette holder
- ○ display by man of abhorrence to conditions
- ○ patronizing stance by woman
- ○ both standing at distance from interviewees
- ○ interviewees appear offended, affronted
- ○ woman sullen, man ashamed
- ○ standing with heads above interviewees

4. TRAINER'S NOTE
○ modest, humble dress, similar to village dweller
○ displays interest in people, pleasant open expression
○ elicits open response from village people
○ crouches (head-level with interviewees)

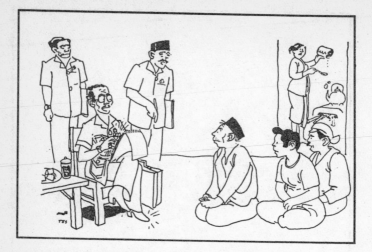

5. TRAINER'S NOTE
○ researcher wearing government uniform
○ ostentatious display of wealth
○ appears to be interrogating – threatening stance
○ interviewing in front of local government personnel
○ elevated position in relation to interviewees
○ threatening posture/confrontation atmosphere
○ location inside villager's house – imposes financial cost of hospitality
○ shoes still on
○ group interview disrupts agricultural work
○ villagers appear intimidated – will try to please/placate

6. TRAINER'S NOTE
- ○ stance of researcher – sitting on ground with interviewees
- ○ open, pleasant expression upon face of researcher
- ○ using opportunity provided by tea break from work
- ○ interviewing at worksite – little disruption
- ○ dress modest, inconspicuous
- ○ scene informal, villagers relaxed, smoking open to talk

7. TRAINER'S NOTE
○ formal, artificial scene – unfamiliar surroundings to
  villagers
○ confrontational lay-out – lines (chairs for visitors,
  benches for villagers like a school, belittling for
  villagers)
○ use of modern technology (speaker/mike) emphasizes
  distance between interviewers and villagers
○ appears to be no dialogue – one-way speech
○ audience appears ashamed, bored, puzzled

8. TRAINER'S NOTE
○ interviewer shares cigarettes
○ talking in coffee shop, informal and inconspicuous (pad on bench)
○ researcher close to interviewees
○ researcher getting interviewees talking

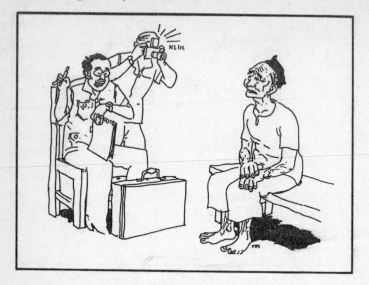

9. TRAINER'S NOTE
○ ostentatious dress
○ photograph intrusion – expensive camera (Was permission asked? How will photo be used?)
○ impatient researcher, anxious to leave, looking at watch, forced atmosphere
○ briefcase as barrier
○ man intimidated, has a perplexed, concerned expression

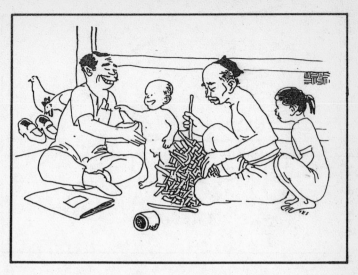

10. TRAINER'S NOTE
- ○ researcher on floor inside villager's house
- ○ has taken shoes off
- ○ oblivious to untidiness (mug on floor)
- ○ informal, non-threatening, patient (plays with baby)
- ○ note-taking interrupted
- ○ pleasant expression
- ○ villagers' work not interrupted

11. TRAINER'S NOTE
- ◯ researcher insensitive to interruption of arduous work of man
- ◯ impatience demonstrated (won't wait for load to be put down)
- ◯ dress, expression, stance – officious and over-bearing

12. TRAINER'S NOTE
○ researcher invites man to have break
○ offers cigarette, builds rapport
○ establishes open, informal, non-intimidating
 atmosphere

14. The Unfolding of the Sarilakas Experience

by Rafael S. Espiritu

This chapter describes the work in the Philippines in 1986 of SARILAKAS and then PROCESS (Participatory Research, Organization of Communities and Education in the Struggle for Self-Reliance). Rafael Espiritu was the Project Director of Sarilakas under the Ministry of Labour and Employment of the gove.nment of the Philippines, and a former member of the PROCESS Board of Trustees.

Origin

SARILAKAS comes from the Tagalog *Sariling Lakas* which means "own strength". It is the code name of a project initiated by the Bureau of Rural Workers in 1981 in co-operation with the ILO and the Dutch government. The project was, in fact, a re-orientation of an earlier project called Project AID (Action Identification for the Development of Landless Rural Workers) which was launched in July 1979. The change in the project's title is more symbolic as the thrust and objective of Project AID had to be radically altered to "focus on providing external inputs of a *catalytic* nature only toward the generation and development of participatory people's processes and self-reliant organizations of Rural Workers".

Project SARILAKAS was evaluated in July 1982 by the ILO, the Dutch government, the SARILAKAS staff and the people themselves. The combined reports of Mr Rahman

Ways of Avoiding the Reality of Poverty

Source: Richard Holloway and David Watson (eds), *Changing Focus – Involving the Rural Poor in Development Planning* (Oxford and IBH Publishing: New Delhi, 1989).

and Mr Veenstra pointed out the significant gains achieved by the project in the field of promoting the rural poor's self-reliant organizations for their own development. On this basis, there was a recommendation to launch a bigger project, but with the strong suggestion that such a project be allowed to operate with maximum operational flexibility. The objective was to free it from the rigidities of the bureaucracy, experience showing that effective catalytic work could only take place if the people's own needs and requirements were given foremost and genuine attention above those of outside institutions (notwithstanding their good intentions).

Guided by this principle and animated by the challenge to continue the task of expanding the strong and democratic institutions of the rural poor as envisioned under ILO Convention 141, the staff of Project SARILAKAS decided to form their own NGO called PROCESS (Participatory Research, Organization of Communities and Education towards Struggle for Self-Reliance) on 6 October 1982. The change did not come easily on the part of the SARILAKAS' staff as they had to persist in their commitment for a period of at least one year with virtually no funds.

Since then, SARILAKAS has continued to be implemented by PROCESS. It is presently supported by the Friedrich Nauman Stiftung (West Germany) and CUSO (Canada) with technical support in the legal area coming from the ICLD (International Centre for Law and Development). PROCESS is governed by a Board of Directors comprising the key actors in the SARILAKAS project, two progressive law professors from the University of the Philippines, and a prominent Filipino human rights activist who was recently appointed by the new President of the Philippines to the post of Ambassador to the Federal Republic of West Germany. PROCESS also has an International Board of Advisers composed of individuals who are strong advocates of genuinely self-reliant people's development. This Board includes the present Chief Justice of India, and ILO official, an officer of the Dutch Ministry of Development, and a professor of law in India.

In 1983, the project covered only a cluster of three villages in Antique and two villages in Batangas. Today, the work has expanded to six municipalities (about 30 villages) in the province of Antique with a target population of 100,000 small fishermen and farmers; 15 municipalities (about 40 villages) in the province of Bihol; any three municipalities (about 15 villages) in the province of Batangas.

The staff has expanded from four in 1983 to a current total of 20, but there are no plans to expand further since the local "folk catalysts" (internal animators) have started to take on a significant part of the work initially under-taken by the PROCESS "community facilitators" (external animators). In effect, the project staff have become core trainers trying to provide catalytic inputs to the newly opened sites while, at the same time, developing contacts with other NGOs which are also operating in the project areas.

Programmes

Values, Formation and Conscientization

At the heart of PROCESS programmes is the permanent catalytic action which takes place at all levels of interven-tion in the project areas. This is the process of "animation" consisting of integration, self-investigation, group action, reflection, and further mobilization. This on-going task of conscientization and practical action has resulted in the training of local folk catalysts who have taken up mobiliza-tion work outside of their own communities. Almost all of the municipalities (each composed of 10–15 villages, each having 200–600 households) in the three provinces have been affected by the action of the people's organizations in the pilot areas and similar interventions are taking place in the new areas with the support of local folk catalysts.

It can be said that while in 1983 the area of involvement was at the level of a cluster of villages, this has been elevated to the present level of the province. Two com-munity facilitators have withdrawn from the original sites and have opened sites in the new areas together with the local folk catalysts and in co-operation with other NGOs.

The strategy for catalytic intervention has shifted

somewhat from community-specific issues to sectoral (i.e., thematic) issues which made wider mobilization possible. In Antique, for example, the people identified the monopolistic concession system in the gathering of the milkfish fry as an issue which affects all the coastal towns of the province. This system, ironically enough, has been allowed by law to award exclusive fishing rights to individuals who could put up bidding fees running from 100,000 to 200,000 pesos, automatically excluding the small fishermen's access to the municipal waters. Since they have no control of the concession, the small fishermen have to sell their catch only to the concessioner at very low prices, at the same time paying a certain percentage of the catch to the same concessioner for fishing within his fishing area.

This oppressive system has been taken up in a provincial workshop arranged by the people's organizations in Tibiao with the support of PROCESS. The people came out with a resolution to abolish the concession system through public bidding which was presented before the governor, mayors and other government officials in a face-to-face discussion. As a result, the officials have pledged to abolish the system in their respective areas. As of June 1986, three municipalities have already institutionalized more liberal arrangements in the granting of fishery rights, giving priority to the livelihood of small fishermen. In other municipalities, the small fishermen are forming their own organizations and are expected to address the same issue with the local government.

Interestingly, the local government officials have been very co-operative with the people's organizations, since most of them have been recently designated by the new government to replace the old governors and mayors elected during the previous regime. In a provincial meeting attended by all the municipal mayors and provincial officials, the governor himself endorsed the work of PROCESS and moved for the approval of the people's resolution.

In the province of Bihol, the people have taken up the problem of illegal and destructive methods of fishing. The unabated use of illegal and destructive practices in fishing have already damaged 70 per cent of the coral reefs resulting in a dramatic decrease in the fish catch of the subsistence fishermen. This exacerbates the growing poverty and restlessness in the various municipalities in Bihol. This issue was found to be significant in that the marine ecosystem of the Philippines accounts for an estimated 1.5 million metric tonnes of fish a year, making the Philippines the thirteenth largest fish producer in the world. (In Bihol alone, there are about 27,993 small fishermen directly supporting a population of approximately 350,000.)

Having seen the dangers of the continuous destruction of marine life, the people's organizations in Tubigon, Bihol (the central site of PROCESS in the province) organized a province-wide workshop attended by representatives of the small fishermen in the different municipalities. As in the Antique experience, the workshop resulted in a declaration of principles and a covenant of action which highlighted the necessity for expanding people's organizations in the entire province of Bihol, and the need to combat illegal fishing through vigilance, land reform and alternative fishing technologies.

Another interesting activity of the organization is the construction of artificial reefs made from used car tyres which are dumped into the sea to serve as a haven for shellfish enabling rock fish to thrive again in areas where corals have been partially or totally destroyed. There is also a strong campaign to preserve mangroves and adopt indigenous technologies for catching fish which do not destroy the marine ecosystem.

In Batangas, the sugar tenants of Taludtod (the central site of PROCESS in the province) have identified the land-tenure arrangement (tenancy) as the basic problem. While the sugar tenants already won significant victories in getting full compliance with the prevailing sharing arrangement, they now realize that the sharing arrangement itself is oppressive and needs to be changed. Recognizing that this goal cannot be achieved without the collective support of other tenants in the province, they decided to mobilize themselves in order to reach out to the other areas. A provincial workshop has been scheduled at the end of this month with the objective of deepening their understanding about sugar tenancy and the alternative courses of action they can take. An effort to document the oppressive character of sugar tenancy is being worked out to serve as an input to the work of the Constitutional Commission which is presently drafting a new constitution for the country.

Economic Self-Reliance

PROCESS believes that people are truly empowered when they gain access to and control over economic resources; when they are able to reduce and overcome their dependencies on forces which exploit them; and when they manage their own economic activities which truly respond to their needs and that of the community. Very often, support groups express their concern in this area by setting up income- and employment-generating projects, more particularly extending credit and other forms of material support. This has resulted in the expansion of the income and employment base of the rural communities but, soon enough, projects begin to suffer from a host of difficulties most often related to management, marketing, and financial accountability. Unless project development is directly linked to empowerment, PROCESS has seen through its own experience that income- and employment-generating projects can be counter-productive, divisive and diversionary.

Hence, in Antique the emphasis is on the abolition of the concession system. This could bring about better price control, the improved marketing of the milkfish, and the adoption of more effective and less destructive technologies. The organizations, of course, implement supplementary socio-economic projects funded by themselves or by outside institutions, but always these activities are undertaken to strengthen further their capacity to gain more effective control over resources in the community.

The organization in Antique, for example, was successful in its fishing project which has a gross income of close to a million pesos a year. The members of the organization were at first euphoric about this performance but they soon realized that so much of their time was spent in managing their project that they nearly forgot about other organizational concerns such as enhancing membership-participation in decision-making, expanding membership, etc.

In Bihol, the people are developing alternative technology schemes while in Batangas, the organizations have started to go with inter- and multi-cropping in the idle sugar lands.

The interventions now taking place in all the project areas have created an impact not only on the values of the people but more so on their economic conditions as they gradually make adjustments to their economic and production structures, and establish self-help income- and employment-generating projects.

The Development of Legal Resources

By and large, the law and the legal system in the Philippines is urban based, colonial and anti-poor, not only in formulation, but more so in practice. The people's organizations have discovered that most, if not all, of the community issues and problems they have are intertwined with law. This explains why the law is seen as a terror and an oppressor, not as a liberator. The law has become an instrument the dominant classes use to perpetuate their interests without regard to the rights of the disadvantaged. The people's organizations have now realized that unless they are empowered, the law will always be an alien and inhuman force. It has therefore become an integral part of the process of the people's organizations to understand the legal issues, the dynamics of law, the limits of legal action, the avenues for "meta-legal action" (different forms of spontaneous collective people's actions), etc.

PROCESS provides catalytic inputs in the form of legal resources, by facilitating the production of practical and simple legal information materials such as primers and comics. Workshops and para-legal education are also being organized in all the project areas. Eventually, PROCESS hopes to develop an alternative legal education curriculum specific to needs of the project sites, and also of the project staff and other social action groups who may feel attracted towards integrating legal-resources development into their organizing strategies.

To promote this strategy, PROCESS has collaborated with a number of law schools to make law students aware of the need for legal resources for the poor. In the summer of 1986, 20 students spent their practicum at the PROCESS sites where they immersed themselves in the villages looking at the problems of the rural poor not from the pages of the law books, but from the eyes of the poor themselves. The result was very encouraging. Four primers on sugar tenancy, illegal fishing, land rights, concession systems, etc., were produced which are now being translated into the local dialect. A number of students have expressed an interest in working in rural communities after qualifying, and almost all want to take up the subject of "Titles" since most of the problems in the communities had something to do with property rights. PROCESS now intends to involve three other law schools which are closer to the project sites.

In support of its work in this area, PROCESS also taps the local legal-aid groups in the provinces and individual lawyers. They are being encouraged to come together as a legal resources support team which could provide legal and extra-legal (e.g., advice on demonstrations and lobbying) advice to the people's organizations. It should be emphasized that the objective is not to supplant the people's initiatives but to strengthen their ability to use the law as a resource. This explains the caution of PROCESS in using the law as a way of resolving conflicts, a fact so easily accepted by most support groups. Litigation is, therefore, seen as only one, and one of the least effective, of the methods that can be used to solve community problems. Part of the educational process is a realization of this fact.

Being a new concern, PROCESS decided to organize a national workshop bringing together legal-aid and social-action groups (including the church and the government) in order to discuss the use of the law in people's empowerment, especially in the light of the new political situation. A journal on legal-resources development was also produced in response to the demand of other social-action groups to see a continuing documentation of the experiences on the development of legal resources.

Community Communications
To be an effective facilitator or catalyst, one must be an effective communicator. Passivity and dependency are not only to be found in the areas of economic and political resources but also, and much more intensely, in the area of knowledge and information. Unless there is a more equal sharing of knowledge, people's organizations will eventually weaken and degenerate into units which can easily be manipulated by forces claiming superiority over the people in terms of knowledge and information. PROCESS believes that people's organizations should have access, control and ultimate ownership of the media and other forms of communications.

At the moment, the people's organizations in Antique

have been successful in negotiating for an hour of radio time with the local Catholic church. In the programme, they discuss their problems and actions. They are now planning to make radio dramas so that the communication of their ideas is more interesting for the listener. The communities are also being trained in community news-writing, drama, and radio production so that they can acquire the skills to produce programmes by themselves. In all the sites, information materials are being translated into the dialect to disseminate important information on a more effective and wider scale.

Afterword
Where to Next? Governments, NGOs, and Development Practitioners

by Richard Holloway

A worst-case scenario

Those who have read that seminal book published by BRAC (the Bangladesh Rural Advancement Committee) in Bangladesh, *The Net*,[1] will be aware of the research it contains which shows almost no political space in the villages in Bangladesh for the poor to improve their lives *vis-à-vis* the controlling powers. I *think* this is an extreme case; if it were the usual pattern, it would seem a recipe for revolution as that would be the only way to change things. In 1989, the poor in Negros in the Philippines, or in Bihar in India, may well feel this way. It is salutary for us to look back at BRAC's analysis, however, before we can look forward more positively to a world in which NGOs and government can work together to assist the poor and powerless. *The Net* gives us a unique insight into the context in which government policies are implemented:

(i) Asia is a region where the economic and political exploitation of the lower classes is both historical and sanctified by tradition. To a large extent, it is accepted by both sides and internalized through the culture. For "development" to provide an opportunity for further extension of this situation is therefore unremarkable. The gains from the harvest for the share-croppers, the interest rate for the money-lenders, the attitudes towards women, and the respect for those who have power, all are old and accepted customs. It is accepted that society is stratified, that there are village élites and the "natural" tendency of those élites is to seek to exploit others. There is of course an implicit limit to such exploitation – when such limits are exceeded or when exploitative behaviour is reinforced by personally insulting behaviour, the whole nexus may be challenged, and the oppressed may feel that what was tolerable becomes untolerable. The outbursts that follow such crises are usually put down decisively by the forces of the state enlisted by the existing élites.

(ii) At a local level, government authority may well be delegated to the village élites and this further sanctions traditionally exploitative behaviour. In most countries in Asia, the village head is a member of the village élite almost by definition. In order to implement development activities, the government will work through the existing structure and re-affirm it. The result will be loyalty from village élites to a government that continues to benefit from them.

(iii) The system is further reinforced by local government functionaries when they work at the village level. Such officials are nearly always co-opted by the traditional power structure with whom they work to mutual advantage, since they are the conduit through which funds for development reach the rural areas.

(iv) The reality, therefore, of government development activities is that they are aimed at middle-level rural peasants because they have resources and because they are traditional leaders. Moreover, such targeting will attract the loyalty of such people to the government. These development strategies are also often claimed to have a spill-over or a trickle-down effect to the poorer people. The people who implement such programmes, however, are the village authorities and the government officials who have mutual interests. Such people are by definition members of the relatively well-off village élites and, not surprisingly, put their own interests before those of the poor peasants. It is too optimistic to believe that they will have an altruistic desire to help the people from whom they extract money to become independent from them.

A more optimistic view

Given this gloomy context, one wonders whether there is indeed any commitment to help the rural poor from the governments of Asia. A common problem is governments having the desire to help, but being unable to do so well. In such cases, if approached diplomatically, government officials can be persuaded of the pragmatic value of involving people's organizations, participatory modes of planning and all the other activities in which NGOs have a lot of experience. In his book *Putting People First – Sociological Variables in Rural Development,*[2] Michael Cernea, the World Bank's Sociology adviser, argues from a pragmatic standpoint using World Bank evaluations that the better projects are done in this way.

Another problem, however, is persuading governments that they should be committed to the specific development of the poor. Hopefully, there are seeds of such commitment in most governments and the following factors may draw more attention to this situation.

(i) The absolute numbers of poor, and the numbers of

poor relative to the rest of the population are increasing in most developing Asian countries. This must be seen by governments as an unstable and politically worrying state of affairs.

(ii) There is a growing understanding that uncontrolled exploitation of the poor produces a kind of "drone" class amongst the élites who expropriate wealth from others but do not produce wealth themselves through productive work and investment. The state, which needs growth and production, can appreciate that a class of people who live by their labour and their ability to produce (i.e., the poor) are more likely to help the state in the long run than those who live by money-lending and surplus extraction. There is also an increasing amount of research which shows that the poor are much better at paying back loans than the well off.[3]

(iii) Existing government programmes which deal with the poor, if they do so at all, are often seen by the governments as a form of charitable welfare. They are expensive and will not go away. An investment which will remove the constraints on the poor and allow them to escape their poverty will possibly free governments from this drain on its exchequer.

(iv) The so-called "development crisis" has meant that there is less aid money around to help governments continue with their existing plans; on the other hand, the increasing amounts of funds which are available via NGO donors start to become attractive to governments. Governments will, however, need to accommodate different ways of working if they want to get their hands on such funds.

(v) The international bilateral and multilateral donor community is pressing governments hard to be more responsive to the problems of the poor, and is pressing them to work with, and accommodate, the methodologies of NGOs. While donor organizations will rarely press their opinions up to the point of threatening to stop aid unless governments work more constructively with the poor, a powerful amount of leverage is possible.

(vi) Governments which, in the past, depended on strongly centralized administrations are now realizing the pragmatic limitations to this. A pattern of decentralizing initiatives are now being seen in many countries in Asia. When the rural population are dealing not with impersonal directives from the capital, but with local government representatives, and when government is trying to implement development activities which cannot succeed without the people's involvement, the need for organizations of the rural poor becomes inescapable. Carefully nurtured, such organizations can be of the poor and for the poor, rather than government creations.

A hard look at NGOs

There is a danger, however, in suggesting that all NGO activities are admirable and worth replicating. A subsequent article by Michael Cernea makes a strong plea for increasing the role of NGOs, as well as for a recognition and demonstration of their great potential as a development resource. He does, however, vividly point out that it is ill-advised to glamorize NGOs and their achievements. They have many weaknesses which to quote Cernea, include

a) Limited replicability. Many NGO-sponsored activities are too small and localized to have important regional or national impact. NGO activities depend on a highly motivated and culturally sensitive staff, and where staff intensity and motivation cannot be replicated, the activities themselves cannot be replicated.

b) Limited self-sustainability. Many NGO-sponsored projects are not designed so that in the future they can sustain themselves with little or no outside aid to the beneficiary communities; this is particularly true when it comes to the long-term maintenance requirements of water and sanitation systems and other small-scale local infrastructure projects.

c) Limited technical analysis. Initiation of local NGO projects often occurs with limited technical feasibility analysis and weak data bases. This is often the result of a lack of sufficient technical, managerial or economic staff/skills, which is understandable given the circumstances of many NGOs, yet affects overall results.

d) Lack of broad programming context. Although it may vary by region or sector, NGO projects often are implemented individually, not as part of a broader programming strategy. Often NGOs carry out their initiatives and projects individually and relatively or completely unconnected with other NGOs or programmes, a tendency that hinders the establishment of country-wide or region-wide programmes.

He goes on to give valuable advice:

It is important, and not belittling, to analyze the weaknesses of NGOs, precisely because altogether they are going through a period of impressive organisational growth which could be steered towards overcoming them. Insightful observers have noted that NGOs are so frequently lost in self-admiration that they fail to see that even the strengths for which they are acclaimed can also be serious weaknesses: for instance in the face of pervasive poverty, "small-scale" can merely mean "insignificant"; "politically independent" can mean "powerless" or "disconnected"; "low cost" can mean "under-financed" or "poor quality"; "innovative" can mean simply "temporary" or "unsustainable".

and then comes to the worthwhile conclusion:

The essential conclusion, in my view, is that the recognition of the key, growing, contribution that NGOs can and do make should not be accompanied by the mistake of idealizing them. NGOs have a great capacity, but they are not the ultimate panacea to the contradictions and difficulties of planned change and induced development. An objective approach to the limitations and weaknesses of NGOs is required for strengthening their own structures and performance, as well as for making their activities technically and economically sounder, and more replicable.[4]

Realistic options

Given this situation, the options for NGOs are:

(i) to look for political space where the poor can organize, look after their own interests, claim their rights from governments, and challenge the control of the village élites and the government functionaries over their lives; and do all this without being smashed. In this case the NGOs' purpose must be to build people's organizations, not to have activities for their own sake.

(ii) to look for alternatives to the existing government systems for delivering resources to the rural poor. When NGOs have implemented and refined such alternatives (and they are seen to work), they must be introduced to government policy-makers with the intention of having them integrated with reformed government programmes which will make their demonstrated benefits more widespread.

(iii) to persuade governments to modify programmes by pointing out inconsistencies, doing research into alternative ways of implementing programmes, and encouraging pressure groups.

(iv) to help governments think differently, act differently, in fact to help create political space by introducing ideas, building coalitions of friends and sympathizers, and looking for points of common interest between governments and NGOs.

For NGOs to get involved in this kind of work requires some re-thinking. NGOs have increasingly been questioning the assumptions underlying their limited development roles and have been wondering how they can change national policy in the directions sympathetic to their own practices and experience. Many of the larger NGOs have become aware of a broader range of possibilities. This awareness has been heightened by the popularization of a simple framework distinguishing between three distinctive orientations in programming strategy by David Korten. All three orientations will be found within a mature NGO community, and sometimes within a single NGO. At the same time, there is an underlying direction of movement that has resulted in the labelling of the three orientations as first, second, and third generation. David Korten's typology is as follows.

Generation 1: Relief and Welfare. Traditionally NGOs seeking to address issues of poverty in the South have been known for their role in the delivery of welfare services – now defined as first generation strategies. This required capabilities in operations and logistics management. While such services may alleviate the consequences of poverty, to the extent they are dependent on outside financing, they contribute little to sustained development.

Generation 2: Small-scale Self-reliant Local Development. In the late 1970s many NGOs undertook to transform themselves from relief organisations into development organisations. The most common outcome was a commitment to community development activities aimed at strengthening local self-reliance – now defined as second generation strategies. Partly because of donor requirements, second generation strategies have featured attention to developing skills in project management. Unfortunately these activities commonly take place in institutional and policy contexts that all but preclude sustainability after the NGO withdraws.

Generation 3: Sustainable Systems Development. A third generation strategy seeks changes in the institutional and policy context consistent with greater local control and initiative. It generally implies less direct involvement at village level for these particular NGOs, and greater involvement with a variety of public and private organisations that control resources and policies bearing on local development. Because third generation strategies depend on positioning the NGO's limited resources to leverage systems that may control hundreds or even thousands of times the amount of its own resources, they imply a need for well developed capacities management.

This framework has become popular among NGOs around the world as a simple device for positioning themselves within the larger spectrum of opportunities, and for defining the nature of their own capacity building needs.[5]

None of these orientations is "better" than the other. I

emphasize Korten's point that a mature NGO will include all three orientations. Disasters will often set up a dynamic in which social structures can be overturned, and relief and rehabilitation judiciously applied can help change the status quo; while projects will be the models in microcosm that can be used to demonstrate to government the possibilities of a variety of ways of working. The capacity to influence government policy will only come when the NGO has developed a track record and some sympathetic contacts inside government as a result of its work in the first two generations. But for expanding the role of NGOs *vis-à-vis* governments so that the valuable work NGOs can do is given a chance of influencing and changing policy, the third generation strategy is needed.

There is also a role here for those who fund development and feel that better development for the poor and powerless would follow greater co-operation between governments and NGOs. There is a large amount of leverage possible through the efforts of multilateral and bilateral funds, and their advisers, as well as, to a lesser extent, NGO funds and their advisers. Their strategy should be to create a climate of opinion in government conducive to NGO efforts and intentions. Some components could be:

(i) strengthening and expanding the work of NGOs so that their efforts can be made more significant, more widely spread, and more visible to governments;

(ii) educating governments about the NGOs and the importance of their work by a sensitive approach to the right people at the right time with the intention of getting governments to take the NGOs' methods on board and make them the official policy; *and*

(iii) fending off interference from those whose interests would be threatened by both of the above, in order to give these ideas a clear field. This means sometimes creating a climate of legal and social opinion conducive to these efforts, and backing them with some legal and political muscle.

If NGOs take up this challenge of the "third generation strategy", they will have to change as well. When high quality work that has been sporadic and isolated is expanded to a national level, many more considerations come into play than the NGOs have had to consider before. The macro-economic situation, policy alternatives, and many other factors have to be considered, and the NGOs may not have the experience and expertise to work at this level.

There are some NGOs who have acquired these skills, however: the issue-oriented NGOs who support and lobby on particular topics such as the preservation of the rain forest, the control of baby foods, seed monopolies, or political prisoners. In many cases, such bodies have worked successfully to change specific government policies in ways that benefit the poor. A good example is the introduction of the new drug policy in Bangladesh.[6] NGOs in Bangladesh have achieved this by demonstrating the efficacy of their arguments, forming coalitions of people inside and outside government, convincing the government of the value of their opinions and experience, proposing alternatives that are workable and acceptable to the government, and doing this in collaboration with international bodies such as WHO. NGOs and their backers who are pushing for a different approach to development programmes for the poor (a much wider task) have a lot to learn from the tactics of those pushing for specific changes in policy and practice.

It seems to be proven that there needs to be better interaction and co-operation between NGOs and governments if the poor and powerless are going to be helped to become self-reliant. NGOs, though of high quality, cannot work on a big enough canvas – governments have the capacity to extend good ideas, and enlarge them to scale but they have built-in limitations. One important limitation is the attitudes and behaviour of those on the bottom rungs of the government ladder. Low-level functionaries who have something personal to lose are likely to derail such initiatives much more than the policy-makers in the capital. Government functionaries do not look upon the rural poor as their clients whom they should serve – their attention is drawn much more towards their boss, the party, departmental policy, and the protection of their own interests.

Always waiting in the wings will be people ready to accuse those working on behalf of the poor of being "subversive", "destabilizing elements", "communists", etc. Where such accusers are powerful people in the village and are able to suborn or control the local police and courts, the NGOs and their followers are likely to be subject to arbitrary arrest and harassment. While it is true that the future of poor-people centred development programmes has to be approached through a fusion of government and NGO practices, it will be far from easy to bring this about when to do so will erode the power and income of the government officials. If, finally, governments and NGOs do decide sincerely to work together, and in a bottom-up manner, there will need to be strong directives down the governmental chain of command and some new systems put into place that make the poor people the final arbiters of whether or not a programme is working, or of whether a project is to their advantage. A *sine qua non* of people-centred development is that they are involved from the start, and they work out whether the proposed programmes will be beneficial to them. Given the way in which government officials practice development at the present, however, even to get to that stage will require a mighty shift in attitudes.

Therefore, bringing together the experiences of those

organizations who have accepted and refined the ideas implicit in the "Third Generation Strategy", the experiences of lobbying and advocacy groups, the experiences of those in government and the international bodies who are sympathetic to NGO approaches, and the experiences of political movements and research organizations, we can begin to define a way forward which will maintain the high quality of much NGO work, and yet allow it to be extrapolated on a national scale so that it really makes a difference to the lives of the poor and disadvantaged. A way forward might consist of the following elements:

(i) to improve the capabilities of NGOs so that they can work at the macro-level, without losing the qualities which made their work important at the micro-level;

(ii) to develop a climate of opinion in government, and the country at large, in which the NGOs' ideas can be well received;

(iii) to gather and demonstrate impressive information on and analysis of the real situation of the poor and powerless;

(iv) to research alternative policy models within which the NGOs ideas would work (and, if possible, graft them onto fertile government initiatives);

(v) to identify those whose interests will be threatened and who will attack the possibility of new policies and "run interference" or fend them off; *and*

(vi) to persuade those in the donor community who have leverage, about the validity and possibilities of new policies, and persuade them to use that leverage.

I can foresee that this will not be an easy task – there would be much soul-searching and agonizing on behalf of the NGOs about compromising their ideas and ideals; and much dissatisfaction from governments as their integrity and commitment are questioned. However, it is important that such collaboration takes place, and that each becomes more familiar with the other – for only then can good work be done on a large scale. We will need to document such cases as they come up and feed the information back to both sides. That way we can refine our skills and get better at doing development.

NOTES

1. The Bangladesh Rural Advancement Committee (BRAC), *The Net – Power Structure in Ten Villages*, Rural Study Series No. 2 (BRAC: Bangladesh, 1983).
2. Michael Cernea, *Putting People First – Sociological Variables in Rural Development* (World Bank: Washington, DC, 1986).
3. The Grameen Bank in Bangladesh, which only lends to the poor, has a repayment rate of 97 per cent, something never achieved by state banks lending to the well off.
4. Michael Cernea, *Non-Government Organizations and Local Development* (World Bank: Washington, DC, April 1988).
5. David Korten "Development alternatives – A challenge for NGOs ", supplement to "Third generation NGO strategies: A key to people-centred development" in *World Development*, Autumn 1987, pp. 145–159.
6. See Dexter Tiranti, *The Bangladesh Experience – Four Years On, 1982–86* (International Organization of Consumer Unions: Penang, 1986).

Index